Pillow Talk

Ricky Boone

Andrea Johnson Books Publishing

Introduction

To start off, I thought I'd tell you just a little bit about me and the things that inspired me, as well as the great people in my life.

Well what started me off were the beautiful writings of Desiree Renea, and my Grandmother Ira Lewis, which both were ministers and poets.

My poetry is written to inspire those who have given up on love, and to let many know that it isn't too late to love, and to never give up on love. My experiences that I share with you in my flow are all facts. I encourage many of you to think outside the box and learn to use the imagination. We all desire to be loved in a special way, and everyone doesn't deserve the type of love that you give.

Throughout my life I've loved two women and was infatuated with two others. However, I've learned a lot from all of them which is what made me the man that I am today. I shed tears from a broken heart from those who weren't ready, and through poetry, which was an escape I created. An idea of what love is really supposed to be.

Poetry can make you smile, cry, want to love and express your anger, etc....Throughout my life, God allowed me to always express myself in many ways, and writing is one of my ways of expressions. Please allow yourself to feel, allow your imagination to run. Step outside the box and let go of everything that bound you in, and just imagine.

Ricky Boone

Acknowledgements

First off, I would like to thank and acknowledge all of those who supported my writings on the media, and followed me from the beginning.

The Mother of my Child who inspired a lot of my writings, Kesha Murphy, and my poetic sista, Kenyan Johnson. Shakieta Robinson, Eric Bryant, Shavon Davis, Ms Hopskins, Montecon Scroggins, Arnesha Banks, Xochi Torres, which is my better half in this poetic world of ink. Bell Williams, Ryan Jackson, Damia Jackson, Andrea Johnson, and Tien Ellis; who stood by me in the ending and helped me push through with all of this, and putting this together. Also, a lot more people and some I wish not to mention, but I was inspired by their stories and also the experiences as well, that motivated me to write a lot of these pieces.

I'd like to thank those for the encouraging words daily that flooded my timeline and inbox, that pushed me to continue my vision and my thoughts, my experiences throughout my love life.

All of these thoughts written were shared to bring and give hope to those who have given up on love. Pretty much 85% of all my writings are straight facts, which are my greatest experiences. Inspired by some of my favorite poets as well: Jacqueline Halmon, Desiree Renea, and Marcus Gray with all the knowledge.

Ricky Boone

Pillow Talk

Cover art designed by Andrea Johnson Books Publishing.

First published by Andrea Johnson Books Publishing. 08/30/2019

6565 N. MacArthur Blvd, Suite 225 Dallas, TX. 75039
www.Ajbpublishing.com

ISBN: 13: 978-0-578-57099-0

Table of contents

Between The Sheets

Are you ready?

Are you ready......
If I kissed you all over your body would you like
that?
Or if I undressed you
Then undressed myself, would you like that?
Do you like when I talk to you crazy,
You never seem to amaze me
Make love til we both can't breathe, so don't be
lazy
This is not a one night stand
but a life time plan. I'm so loving the way you
love me, so tonight's all grand.
Candle lights while watching our shadows dance
Ice and pop sickles, cherries and hot nickels.
Girl I'm so excited if you came a little closer,
you'll see me shaking.
Just to see you naked was something that I've
always imagined.
And I'm thinking about putting a ring on it.
It a only be right if I'm always on it.
I want to value you
I'm different
because girl I'm everything you've been missing.
Listen while we switch positions
We modern, this ain't tradition.

Close grippin, no time for slipping
Our souls are shifting.
I'm not like other men
I'm deep in your brown skin.
Give me something I can splash and dive and
pound in
Would you like that?
You can fight back
Yes, insight that
Here's a pillow, you can bite that
Brown skin beautiful
Did you write that, top that, drop that
Back fat like that...I like that
Oweeeee now put the dress back on love
Just so I can.... wife that
Because I love you
This is what I loved most about you

Bath water

Can I be the water in your bath?

The anger in your wrath

The sizzles through your cheeks

The warm lavender that soothes you weak

The smile on your face when you tell me how good I taste

The sun you see when you awake

The moans through the love we make

Can I be the running water that you run?

Come and get you some

The running water that makes you numb

Tell me no more, here I come

Step right into me and sit down slow

Watch me rise quickly

Causing an overflow

Running over unto the ground, I just love the sound of all your ooowwww and ahhhh's

Yes love can we drown

Bubbles bursting everywhere in all your secret places love, I can't Maintain it

I'm hypnotized with all your seductive faces

Please don't drain me now

Just let your body soak so please don't lose no hope,

just tell me how far are you willing to go. Lord knows just don't tell me no

Because I'll lose control

Just grab a hold rub me down, I promise no one here will know

And as the bubbles fade away I'll cool down,

but I am here to stay

Fall asleep in me

In every single way, and as soon as you step out of me, I'll put you fast asleep.

But please don't dry me off, let me air dry you til complete.

Can I be the water in your bath?

Pillow Talk

My love will make you splash

My love is an overflow

I'm the bath you've never had.

Can you still feel me?

Yes.....she hardly even knew me. There was no anticipating to do me.

Last night was more than a movie, afterward she would go to sleep,

By me rubbing her booty.

No towels for the wet spots, cold fan cause it gets hot.

I was out of breath cause her spirit had my soul in a HEAD lock

Yes, the bed rock

I had her body tossed in the wind, call me Hancock.

She said my name like a chant

Call me Buddha calling all stops

She couldn't run, little body built for impact

Biting down on the pillow.

Boone the best and that's a darn fact

She'll remember every bit of me and every inch

Tears from a Grinch

I didn't mean to bring out that aggression
Tension,

I zoned out a lot of times just to listen to her
moan, shhhhhh just listen

I can still hear her.... ooohhhh Ricky

I know that thing miss me

Funny

I kept her sticky

There were no complaints I gave her plenty

Of love like high grass

In the deepest forest

Our bedroom was a jungle

Filled with echoes who could ignore it, she crave
my blade, body splashed like a

Village

In a Nile of resurrected graves

I can still feel the trim

The explosion the release got d$%3n!!!

She feel me at this very moment

Oooweeee!!

Can you still feel me?
What's for breakfast now?

I can only picture you

I can only picture you doing to him all the
things you used to do to me. Funny how we used
to love and wake up again to do it all over then
back to sleep.
I got the keys and the rings to the Jeep
Just remember to short me on that square
Whenever you begin to think deep.
Purple roses, I can remember you proposing,
But nobody knows this.
I kept you changing the sheets
From the puddles
Of cold creek, bragging to your people about how
I kept your soul weak.
Don't stunt on me like you don't remember
It was a little bit before December
Your dishes never got cooked,
and out of all people you go and get quick
tempered.
Chili in the morning don't forget the crackers,
Can I touch you before the day start?
Don't worry, we won't miss the rapture.
Singing to your soul with my foreign
instrument

that kept you coming.
Harmonizing with your lips,
Paralyzing my spin as my eyes rolled to the
back of my head.
Body so dead.
As I continue to fill her up over and over again.
All of me
Don't front on me
You know how I did you
You know how I loved you
Love became a sin
It was so good,
the first night it was so hood,
that later on that morning
You was telling me you loved me,
that's when I was told you wasn't my soulmate.
Soulmates don't fall in love,
We would have connected regardless of the
situation.
Due to if you can fall in love you can fall out of
love.
Soulmates can't do without one another.
Without me you should of felt suffocation,
I would of and should of been your air,
More than my deep penetration.
Don't front on me

Now you want to play me for a sucka.
Tell me one thing like
I still love you, but behind my back say another.
But I thank you so love....
I learned to value me more love.
My value is more then what you've viewed in a
brother's pocket.
I have something you'll one day realize you've
had, but will never have.
And it's more than all of me that I've put in you,
and more than what he could ever spend.
Someone who would have breathed for you,
interceded so true.
Someone who would of loved you even if the
limbs would have started falling off.
I would of caught those tears
that fell, and the only time I'd ever make you
cry,
Is whenever I looked at you.
Or when we made love
to a lullaby.
If you only knew...
but you'll never know now.

I'm coming back for you

I'm coming back for you this time and I won't
hold out
If he slip, he bet not trip cause I'm a grip
all of you, I'll never pull out.
Waiting for your call
so if he fall
you know my number, I want not half but all.
I stand tall.
 why you playing, I'm just saying I'm where
your heart should be, he didn't know what he had
until you left, now got you stuck on repeat.
Turn the music up that's our song,
 let me sing it to you all night long
Kiss you at the same time I'm in you,
I gotta crave and it's you on my menu.
Do you know what type of love that you're
facing?
Make love to you til you burn out straight
cremation.
Just be patient, yes I'm praying.
There's no delaying
you can feel me from a distance, you can still
hear the words I be saying.
No I'm not a dreamer, you can still feel me
pulling your hair while your sucking my
fingers.

Hand around your throat kissing you so you'll know I want you baby for life.
Loving you so right
This right here a make you want to be my wife.
You don't have to trust me, I got over 100 people baby that can vouch for me.
So just relax and lay down on this couch for me, I don't smoke, but one hit of me is like you smoking on a whole ounce of weed.
Close your eyes as I use your juices to breathe, I breathe off you, I inhale, yes I gotta get high off this.
I put money on it, if I don't make you mine at this moment you will remember this....

I'm coming back for you

Love you like me

She kept my soul hot like a boiling pot, she was
poetry to my soul my fantasy my Jill Scott. Late
nights she kept me on point getting me right,
Body rippled like waves when she throw love
back, OOoooh what a sight.
Thick like Kelly, and it moves like jelly.
Last night she paid the Price.
It Was a nice night.
Wishing I could love you seven days a week
With no towels on the bed sheets
You can never forget about me
He and whoever may have your mind,
But I'll always be In your heart.
That will always be mine
Lifetime love of mine
When I sparkle you shine.
I value you so.
God made you for me
That's why I sucked the soul out of your body
You are a part of me
I will love you til my dying day
Physically and spiritually you'll forever be a
part of my DNA.
This is more than a complex or just sex
Who can love you like me?
Nobody

Like Keith Sweat
You're my my my my
My sunny days in the rain
Locked into my brain
A memory that just won't fade away.
I don't want no interruptions
When it comes to you
My love is true to you
And I thank God he's blessed me with you
Because can't nobody love me like you do
I'm so so so into you.

I WAS BUILT TO SLAY

She couldn't speak my language,

But she claimed she knew me.

She found there was more to me, than her flossing her breast, and that big donkey booty.

I craved the mind like fine wine; I needed conversation like prime time.

I needed someone who could caress my thoughts, like the food we eat

At the same time run it classy, but keep it nasty

When she touching all over me.

She's the wife type, not a one night.

Gives me insight by the moonlight

And then there's nights,

Nights that we don't even have to physically make love.

We hold each other, and due to the connecting, we stay constantly, mentally making love.

I'll run through her dreams while she plays in mine.

Then we'll wake up, early morning

and blow one another's mind.

We'll play little games like pretending when we first met, take a few shots of Bacardi

For a buzz, then go all in.

Isn't that something?

She'll be my best friend

We'll sing together old school songs, even if she cannot sing

I'll suck on her bottom lip

To press her buttons

Until she begs, "Oh my God, come get me king!"

I'll cry in her lap

When I'm down and hurt,

She'll sleep on my chest,

Knowing she'll always be first

I'll taste her soul while dreaming of paradise,

Then wake her up in heaven,

While her body dripping from heaven's ice.

I'm so exclusive

Trust me when I say this

There's nobody like me, and she knew it

I was built to slay.

Tell me I do

Mentally I'm alone right now
And I can only picture you feeding me into your
zone right now
Baby I need to escape
I need to escape this reality I'm in at this very
moment
I need you to pull me out right now
Right into your world
As I close my eyes and begin to fantasize
You doing all the things I love
And I don't even have to ask because
you know me
And you know me well
I'm loving what you have on
Baby sing to me my favorite love song
Sing to me through your body
Harmonize with me through my soul
Take control
Keep me swoll
Swallow every bit of me
Drown me into your pacific deep
Be my jazz Rib
Love me infinity
Chase me into your dream and out of this
nightmare of make believe
I love you

Keep me closer than most
Yes, you know me...
Oh my God
She's my mental my air in understanding
She listens and watches
Love so classy
When people see you, they see me and when they
see me, they see you
I don't want to wake up
I don't want to finish writing you
I don't want to finish enlightening you
I can feel you now
I can taste your soul on my lips
Don't run...
But I know you can't help it
I'm fun and I bet you right now through these
words you've felt it
I know you
Like you know me...
I am poetry
Don't I taste so sweet...
Tell me I do...

The perfect picture painted

Don't play like you don't remember all those late night traps we use to creep off with

Isn't that something? I bet you never would of thought I had that magic that

Static

That butterfly effect

That had you catching flashbacks

Just like that

Owwee you know you good at what you do...

Let me give you a call, hey what you doing, what time you get off work?

You know what I want to know

Quit playing and hear what I'm saying

The kids are sleep we can creep for about a week

If you're in heat

You can just pull up, shhhhh... don't speak

Yeah, I'm funny dangerous

Stop playing with me

Lava lamp got the room lit up

You got skills

I see you don't toss up

Tattoos on your back and your navel pierce

I see you like to play with ice

Slippery tongue in my ear

I don't fear

Pretty eyes, you a dangerous girl

But I'm a dangerous guy

And play in a sexual world

We all need love you know the number

I paint a picture

Of your full figure

Now watch me grow

And let the pillows talk

And watch our shadows grind on the wall

ooweeee

You got the alcohol in your system

Just a bit wine

I'm a shine through your mind and define

What is blessed

And rest in your finesse

Remember me, I know you do

I remember the body shots with ice

She got a gift that snatch and twist souls like
voodoo

At night

Can I paint a picture?

Paint a perfect picture with words that a hit'cha

She already knows what it is the second she hits
my room

Hits my front door

I'm a need, and not her want

She didn't think I would ever be so serious until
the U turn was made and I made

Things firm

And fulfilled her curiosity

I paint a picture, a perfect picture

A picture painted without a brush

But with a soul

That painted the perfect portrait

Ooowee

As she opens the door with her victorious secret on

After a few shot s taken down

I can't believe I'm laying her down

Oh my God what is this?

Picture painted

The pillow talking

Can I show you something?

Wishing that I could show you what I picture
whenever I close my eyes

Time flies whenever you're having fun

But the sun is going down

I'm wanting some,

So I close my eyes and I begin to picture...

Picture your figure on top of me

Framed in a gold frame

Drained from all the paint that painted you in

Ooweeee, imagining me covered in you

Oh yeah, I got a little thug left in me

but I'm a gentleman first,

But still liable to give you everything you need

No need to plead

I got that antidote to make your soul bleed

But as for right now

Can I make your pillow talk to me?

Giving me all the conversation

To fulfill my needs

Can we dream the possibility?

Let me tell you how much you could mean to me

Oowwwee this isn't me, I guess this is

The pillow talking

Tonight

Tonight's surprise

I like surprises

You've got me excited

Loving the way you're so into me

Now I'm up on 10

You've got me into this feeling

And I needs some healing

A sexual healing

I'm usually a gentleman

But tonight it's a bit different

Due to my adrenaline

Can we get a little crazy tonight?

I'm betting I'm a cure your thirst

Because the feeling so nice

Can I see what's under your skirt?

Like I said, I like surprises

And I can tell you're excited

Come a bit little closer, I just want to show you something

It's time to get fed

Am I all in your head?

No need to lower our tones, we're all alone unplug the phones

We're both on our grown

I got some eggs

Bacon and grits and batter in the morning

So when we get up, I can feed you your second meal if you're still hungry

But as for right now

I know you have a different type of appetite, so lower the lights I'm a get you

Right

You're a little bit tense, it's a gentle bite

God ordained this kiss

Oooowee, your love lock tight as a fist

I'm so excited like it's something I missed

I can't wait to finish just to start again

Love like you make me feel like I'm in love again

   I'll let you take full control

But once your body fold

I'll take control from the backseat

   As long as you're letting go

I'm doing doughnuts, loving you on cruise control

Pray that your extensions are sowed in tight

Because by the end of the night, they'll be lost off into the sheets on the floor

   Due to the love we made sweet, whispering more

Baby I love this black love that we have

We Breathe....

We breathe......

We're going to do this thing different...

So baby listen

I couldn't imagine myself breathing without you not even at a distance

You are the breeze when I'm in need on a hot day, you are a soul I love

I could never hate, you are the eyes for me when there's things I cannot see

That taste I need when I crave sweets, when I can't sleep

Let's drown out our past because you're not her and he's not me

I don't want a repeat

Let's go strong let's go deep

Let this love be an evolution breaking the masses to eternal fusion

Splitting moons

And burning out suns

Let's create another heaven

Where there's no such thing as hell

But sweet waters ran like honey from a
honeycomb

I don't want to play with You no more

The other women before you can't compete

Due to we have each other's minds

Which is the switch board to the body

Breathe on me......

While I breathe into you

Grind on me...

While I stir gracefully throughout you.

Love me slow

But do it in slow motion

Tell me you want more...

And our love will overflow

Can I be your gift?

Can I be your shift!!?

Can I be what lifts you high up off the ground

Leaving you numb

And forgetting where you came from

You are here with me

Our love is like no other

We breathe...the same.... air

You in her

Oh God can you create a love...like
this...Ooweee...She could feel and as well tell that
I've been through some things throughout my
life

that just wasn't right

That could read in between the lines, feed my
spiritual insight

her approach is not like other females

she has a strong foundation not like most that I
attract, that has beautiful hard seashell scales

That cover their true image, which is none,
identifying with the spirit similar to jezebel

Controlling, manipulating

But oh no not this lady

She's not trying to entice me

or just one night me

or rush me into something that could hit a heart
harder than lighting

I need a new air to breathe

you see,

she's possibly what I need

I need...a love that intercedes and a put pressure on my wounds whenever I bleed

She understands me and when she doesn't, she asks

She doesn't fly off like a savage and point out my bad

When I hurt, she hurt and when she hurt, I hurt

And when she thirsts, I'm her ice water

And when I'm hot, she's my cool breeze

She's my vision, I'm her dream

And when I'm wounded, God you give her the strength to help and heal me

She's everything a wife was meant to be

She was built for this

Her eyes see clear through my inner me

She sees my enemies

Her beauty's my epitome

Can I truly have this?

But fix me first so that I don't lose this

Let her scars be sealed as well as mine

Cause true love in this generation is so hard to find

I see her now, but I'll rather wait

Because if I move now, she'll fade away

And I know you'll make a way

if I don't stray away

She won't touch me, but mentally and spiritually love me

She'll stimulate my mental so simple

To the point we'll be reborn into one another through you

Can you create me you, in her?

Your place

There's a part of you that I just can't let go

A part of my soul that just refuse to grow

I thought I'd just let you know that part of me, I wish you could just give it back to me,

 You may be with another across seas, or the river plans, you may be as far as mars or Pluto, it's something I just thought I'd let you know.

That part of my heart you'll always have, and I wish it was some type of way that you could give it back

I don't care where you go

And the trials that you go through

You'll always have my heart

Until God places something into me new

This thing in me refuses to bury you

Your smile your face, the way you look at me, your grace,

The way you say my name

The way you put my fire out whenever I'm in flames

You made me feel I could do everything all over again

And not complain

As long as it was with you

But now I must carry on, sit and write about this thing called love

It's so hard to paint a picture

When all I see is your figures

I miss you

Since you died, I died

And these rivers dried up inside

I just wanted you to know you'll never be forgotten through my mind

These wonderful words paint beautiful pictures of you

Now I know to never take love for granted, that's one thing that I learned from you

No one could ever take your place.

Your Smile

I love the way I make you smile, turn the music low a bit so you can hear me talk about you baby

you're not fine or sexy, but beautiful and just maybe...

maybe we can have a sip of wine and sit up and stare into one another's eyes, and read each other's mind, and say all the things that stimulate our imagination into play

It's been awhile I can tell since you felt this way, what you want to sip on, Moscato patron

Or some Crown to take home

We can light the fireplace so I can watch the flames reflect from the smile on your face

Put that little red sexy thing on

And tie your hair up and put on some HER

Or maybe some Joe or old school like Levert

You would like that won't you?

It feels good cruising late nights up the street

Pillow Talk

I can't wait til I get you home to do what you've grown to love from me

Like rubbing your booty to put you to sleep

I love it when you smile at me

Let me sing to you my remembrance

So that you won't forget

Let me be the reasons to the pieces picked up

That was scattered from the stupid men from your past thrown up

They didn't know what they had

But baby I do

But you don't really know as well what type of love I have that's standing before you

Can I love you just in case this is a season?

So that you can get this experience

Of this meaning

Ohh my, I love it when you smile

I wish I could wake up to it forever

It's so sweet, like yams with crush sweet jiffy cornbread, I love your smile and the way your face ball up and fold up and the way you say daddy

I love to watch you in your sleep watching you smile due to me

When you smile my soul smiles, you just do something to me that makes me feel complete

And if this is a dream, let me sleep forever

Because I know no one has ever possibly made you smile more than me

I love you

After Midnight

Dream about me

You're there with him possibly thinking if you're really what he wants

giving him Chance after chance, heart pounding like crazy praying that you're all he needs and what he really wants

Wondering if you messed up walking out on what was blessed

Knowing I got that magic, that happy off in you, just confess

Just to chance it with you I would live, for in your tenderness every time I see you girl my heart pounds, I just can't rest

and I feel you tied to my soul

and what I gotta know is, do you think and dream about me?

Flashbacks on all the nights we shared

Baby you know you still feel me there

I can be anything you want and all you dream, just speak it and I'll be there

You know my words a fact

If you left now, I'll take you back

I don't know what it is, I guess that Juice Box was just raining like that

I'm so off focus baby

it's like I'm going crazy

girl it's been so darn long

But you know this love I got is so strong, it's something that you do to me

Don't lose out on this great opportunity

And I got to know with this seed I sow, is do you think and dream about me?

I gotta a type of love that a show you

That he can't love you like me...

You'll never get enough I'll swim deeply

If you need me

so just breathe me

I got enough love

So love let me take you right there, so give yourself into me

Baby you got me wide open

And I hope you really notice your chosen

So do you think and dream about the love that
we used to share, when we were laying and
leaning on the kitchen pavement and cabinet?

And what I used to do and how I used to do

And what you're used to me doing

Owwee I want you so bad

Cause I still love you, I do

Baby no matter who you're with or where you at
and love, I gotta know

And yes, I want you so

Do you dream and think about me?

Dream of me

Do you dream of me?

I know you do because I dream of you and all the things we used to do

I'm missing your smile and classy style

And the way you talk to me it's been awhile, we were the perfect match

And just maybe one day I'll have you again, and love you as if I'm trying to get a baby, and I know it sounds crazy but baby that's me

My imagination goes far beyond us just having dreams, I am poetry

Hear my words and hear them loud and clear, when I speak you manifest and appear just right here

I can feel you touching me the very second I close my eyes

And you can probably feel me kissing you between your thighs, tasting your mind

Do you dream of me?

That's all I ask

I dream of you baby wishing love would have last

I can still hear your laugh telling me to stop,
taking your thoughts to candy land

The feeling is yet soft

Tell me you love me just one more time

But be careful when you say it

Because I'll poison your mind to making you
mine

I'm nowhere seductive, but I am about that action

My thoughts a play off, then on my couch you'll
be maxing

Don't tell me you love me, not even in a dream

Because you might just wake up due to your
running stream

Don't tell me you love me, because your heart a
hurt tomorrow

You'll crave what you can't have, and my time
you cannot borrow

Don't tell me you love me then stare out my window, because then I'll have your soul laying in tears on my pillow

Dreaming of me even though I'm right there

Dream of me

He isn't me

He ain't me and you know it ...

Damn...baby do you really know how hard it is for me to even look at your picture?

To even see you with another nigga?

I can tell you ain't happy you just settled because that ain't the same smile I put on you

He ain't doing you like I do you, can't say my love didn't get in and out through you

Ain't nobody stirred them grits up and buttered them biscuits like me boo

I bet you think of me on all the times I had you running, keep the door lock love, due to once I cool down, I'll be back coming

Early morning sun you raining on the sheets

No towels on the bed, now we laying in cold wet spots for nothing

Wash up and put on my favorite dress so I can watch you walk, make you smile, I love the way you walk and talk

Does he tell you you're beautiful every morning?

Open up the car door for you, make you scream whenever you want it?

Make you feel like flying, keep you screaming like you dying

Keep the doors locked, I haven't finished exploring all your hot spots

Keep the lights dim, light up your fireplace

I can still see the big smile on your face

And I know you remember the Taste; due to every darn night I would feed you this gravy with steak. You know I'm a gentleman with class, but you learned I could be a lil aggressive and nasty too

I know you think about me because I think about you, our souls are tied

You just went back to the old and was scared of this brand new

And if you could turn back, I know you would

Your heart is now complicated to these new pictures you see

Because you knew my love was true

And your heart was weak

You'll remember me I guarantee

If it's not my taste or the air I breathe

You'll remember my flow with my stroke

Or the way I made you smile, that feeling of love
that gave you hope

That warm feeling in your throat

That made you think growth

He don't make you smile like I do, I can still feel
you

I can still taste you

It's so sweet

 I can still smell your perfume on my sheets
when I close my eyes, I can still see the tears run
from your cheeks

You wouldn't let me be the reason....

Pictures of me make you weak

And I know it's hard

Trust me I know,

see no matter where you are or at

I'm a forever make love to your soul

Here's where you freak up at....

Letting me in to touch you

Where he left cold

You know he ain't me

Hood rat

What do you do,

when the person you love,

 turns their back on you?

Lies...

Then falls back on you?

Promises that you thought,

would never be broken,

fall through the cracks,

 and make you question,

if their love was even true

Tears hinder my pillowcase with memories,

of her face.

A face I felt,

 I couldn't replace.

She walked away into someone else's arms,

like I never existed.

And she did no harm?

what about all the things I've done that he
couldn't do?

Which is why you came to me

What about the love I've shown

when I'd comfort you,

pray for you while you slept

what about the love I made

when you'd high five my crave

 left the sheets wet

and I drained you

day by day

What about the mental pain?

I loved and tried to cure you,

when you were down,

missing your loved ones,

I was there.

I was that comfort, that shade...

I'm the reason you're pushing,

 what you're pushing,

Sleeping on my Cushion.

I loved you more than life.

But his blunt smoke, alcoholic breath and aged skin,

took the love you felt away

 He can't do you like I do,

and you know it...

I gave you a real family,

but you blew it.

We welcomed you with open arms and open doors,

 but you settled for less,

when I tried to give you more...

Pillow Talk

You got what you got from me
then turned away.
you used me like the last lovers,
you had back in the day.
You burned my heart,
then fell apart.
When I gave you the chance,
Your move wasn't smart.
Why?

But that's okay,
you got what you deserve,
And got what fits you.

My love was too deep.

I was too realistic.

I should of left you

in the streets,

where I found you.

But it was too late...

I fell in love with a hood rat.

And that's one thing I hated was a...

Hood rat.

I woke up

She said she was digging my vibe and she loved the way I think and talk

She couldn't imagine how raspy my voice had sound

and that it didn't fit my face and that is was soft not loud

I told her, well enough about me, and that I'd rather hear about you

She told me she loved soft music and to cuddle and that her favorite was seafood

Old school had no rules

When it came to being compassionate

Old school had no rules

When she told me that I was going to need a seatbelt, best believe I've fastened it

She fed my mind and it was a lot of times

That I didn't even have to touch her

She kept me on my grind

And was so Divine

baby had that snap back that had me sensitive to
the tip

That kept my stroke game on a high

She made my hunger for hustling double

I kind of put things together, I figure different
lovers bring out different things

She wasn't drunk or a jump off

She was classy with a little bit of something that
could rub off

I mean I have never had a lover like this before

She had me feeding her out my plate and
opening up car doors

I put her first in everything I did

It wasn't one time that I didn't think of her,

Slow dancing by the candlelight in her bedroom

Making love on her bearskin rug with the ice and
the lotions too

She had me thinking and doing and trying out
some old and brand new

Oh yes old school knew exactly what to do

What was mine was hers and what was hers was mine

We never cared to watch time

We lived life to the max

Each day was played day by day

Each day was as if two months

Old school love wasn't for no joke

Breakfast was her, before work

And dinner was her, most times after church

She didn't smoke too much, but when she did

It was a high

That made us hold hands and dance on the clouds of rain

I had a woman

I finally actually had a woman

I loved to wake up in the morning to my soul being restrained out of my sleep, when I didn't even have to ask,

I loved going to work just to end the day to get home to her

Due to I finally had a woman

Gorgeous fine and beautiful, she was mine

And guess what......beeep beeep beeep beeep beeep beeep beeep....

I woke up

Looking back

Looking back on things that I didn't know
thinking that I lost the best of women

That they didn't really give me the chance to
grow

Or a chance to sow, but now look at me, that
chance is no

Now I may not be all that, and pockets aren't fat,
but my brain capacity is loaded

With wisdom and hardcore facts

but most of all I'm no dummy

I learned how to love me

And if I can't love me, how can I love you?

It's going to take a lil bit more than just seeing
you bent over with your Tongue hanging out,
looking like jump off in the clubs with no reality
to life,

Looking like all you do is turn up and bang out

 naw naw baby

I dig a lady, not that black Barbie

I'm not that Lil wheezy, and it's going to take more than just head to please me

Real men like me and what I've grown to be don't like it too easy

How about some wine and a pillow, a cool breeze with some conversation chilling?

Looking out an open window

Me touching you

You touching me

Me saying some of the things you've deserve to hear, that you've never heard before

Allow me to listen and study you

I'm that long term

Before he was your lesson learned

We can even pray together when you're down or when you're sick

We can even pray together before we make love asking God to make every stroke

Perfect

But that's something a lot of women aren't used to

Because they had no patience to allow us to sow or even grow

Or maybe they're just being patient with the wrong type of Kats

Thinking that they'll change

By passing up real ones like so....

The pictures painted of me should display a lot

I raised a child that wasn't even Mine for 16 years as my own, and is now grown,

Like many other men has stepped in

And done

And there's many men that are fathers who love and take care of their children

With bitter baby mothers

Who raises hell into their lives just because things didn't turn out so bright

In their lives

Because they're putting in time with the wrong Kats, and the ones they looked at as boring and weak, they didn't have that patience to allow him to grow....

Now he's out there

And he's outgrown you

Looking for that woman that was never in you

I have matured from that Kat to a king because I have grown

And through experience, men such as myself knows how to love,

From experiencing with women,

With no clue

Who play like life is brand new

Who stay praying for Brand new

I thank you for watering me and my roots

because I've grown into knowing not to Love like you

A Chance Again

I tried to walk past her, with my head down, as if I didn't recognize her

She responded, "Oh you gonna play like you don't see me?"

And with the stupidest look on my face, I replied with, "Naw, man how you doing?"

"I'm ok." she replied. Me, I'm thinking about all the lies I've told her to get from up under the relationship, it was merging in like, oh my God she looks good now

Well she was gorgeous then

I just didn't know what to do with that type of woman

She was on a whole different scale then and still elevating now

She was more firm and knowledgeable in her colored skin

More than ever

Sexy, classy and clever

Something I haven't found ever since I dropped her

What was I thinking?

I was a young, dumb minded guy that was thinking about nothing but getting fed

I was in her bed, thinking with the wrong head

Blind-sided, thinking that I found something better, but what did I do...let her go

Darn dummy, wow I was off then

And now it's funny, because she knows why I'm walking around with my head down like a dummy

Thinking about where we could have been, from way back then, til now.

I guess this is just one of those mistakes us men mainly make in life, before we so-call get it right

We mess up and bypass Mrs. Right

And pick up a few helpful wrongs

To get us some experience,

That can help us, or damage us if we don't learn from it

"You don't have to walk around and play like you don't see", she replies

I responded "You look good. How've you been? How's life treating you?... I've heard you've gotten married... and had a few kids, that's awesome."

"Kids are a blessing"

"Your husband made an awesome choice, you're a good woman."

She responded "Thank you very much"

And "Yes indeed he did,

"but you were one that didn't think so"

And she smiled

I smiled right along with her and answered, "Yeah, I messed up, but hey I was young and wild, and didn't know the things I know now,

and if you weren't married, I would offer dinner and maybe a little outing, but I don't do married women because those vows go deep sweetie."

And she laughed

And said, "Who said I was still married? I have children, but it's complicated."

I responded "Really?"

And leaned over the rail and said "Well, can I get you anything to Drink?"

And with a big smile she batted her eyes and said "Yes, a lil' bit of that peach Cîroc and sprite on ice."

And I respond, "How nice."

And replied to the bartender, like that's what the lady wants

Peach Cîroc, sprite and ice.

Spark another square

Turn the heat down for a moment and turn the fan on low...

Due to it's getting a little hot in here and I know in the next five minutes you're going to want a little bit more...

Short me on that square move the ashtray

Right there (beautiful) cover up a bit, let me lock the doors just in case someone decides to run along up in here

I love it when you kiss the tip of my remote control to your soul and

Look me in my eyes and say, baby we going to grow old

As I grasp a hold

To your shoulders like ohhhhh

Blowing the smoke up into the air

As I watch you turn over and arch love up in the air

Like you didn't care, dumping the ashes to the side of your bed as I look down on your ocean, ripples clutching your dimples, holding, pulling so tightly to your hair.

Then my hand is on your neck, let's go, it's so simple

I can still hear you...

So turn the fan up

So you a big girl, quit Running, now go on and man up, put it right there.

You making me stand up

Too bad there are no handcuffs

Turn the music up

before the kids hate us

Pepper sausage and some pancakes would be nice, watching you eat out of your cup of ice

After making me feel so right

Now my stress gone away

Here's shorts on that square, see I almost forgot about you

Come and give me a kiss (beautiful) Oooweee

You hit the spots

So here's half of what I got

Until you come get the rest

You're so beautiful in the morning, and don't let no one tell you different, and if they do trust me, they don't know all that they're missing

And if we ever part, this is what you will remember of me,

I was a true Love lost, something you couldn't see that was meant to be

Short me on that square

The last letter

This will be the first but last time I write you
There's been a lot of things that I always wanted
to say, but now I have the guts to say it without
delay

I'm not trying to disrespect you
Or cause any problems, so make sure you throw
this letter away as soon as you finish reading
this through

I know it may sound selfish, but I have a fetish
The moves we made was selfish
But the love we made was savage
Trust me, I'll keep what took place between me
and you

It a forever be on the low
I'm good at keeping secrets love, ain't nobody
gotta know

What he don't know won't hurt him
But I know you feel bad

Pillow Talk

Because you say you love him
Your heart was and is confused

But you were abused
By a fool who broke all the rules to your heart
And I was there to heal it
I took your mind off of him
But I couldn't take him out your heart

I know and knew that you had a man
But at this moment me writing you I can
careless if he ever found out about me,
But I'll respect you, I'm
Praying that he makes a mistake
So unforgettable
That the love fades away, and whatever seemed
happy goes to sad, So that I can have you back
in every way

Things shouldn't of never been the way that they
are now, Out of respect I'll break away for awhile,
Just when you heal keep me in mind,
You'll be fine, hopefully mine
So that I can hold you down
Just remember to dispose of this letter

Once you finish reading it
I hope you could feel the meaning
And believe it
But I guess I don't know love
Heartbreaks a make you grow up
Love a make you sometimes feel sewed up
We only have one life to live
And I thought I'd just write, due to all this love I
got to give

I can see you with your lips all poked out, eyes
rolling to the back of your head as you continue
to read this
Looking over your shoulder
I didn't want to text it, I didn't want to email it
So I'd rather old fashion it

Paint a picture of me putting my brand on it
making you smile
Cause how I stand on it
You and I were meant
But I'll have to respect it
You were my reflection
The epitome of my erection
You should be here waking up next to me

Instead we creep every other week
When we used to be lovers

Now we're undercover
Chasing one another
And you know we can't be friends
So why bother
It's so hard for me to say hello
Whenever I see you in the public eye
Fear of forever made the door that I hate close cry

But I'll respect it

When it comes to love

When it comes to love, maybe I always attracted
women that allowed me to put my love into
practice
now I've mastered those lessons, now I need a real
love that's more like a friend rather than a
distraction
She can add to me rather than subtract from me
baby, the sound of her is a crave that makes me
want you daily
I need you off my mind and on top of me right
now and yes today
I'm so sick of dreams, I need you here with me
I need her closer than any woman has ever been
next to me before
So close that I can taste her soul with my tongue
with my mouth closed
It can't no way possibly get no better than
this...her kiss...
Is not a wish
 but a blessing that I ask for, lord knows I
deserve this
She takes whatever in my past
And makes it not exist
She's it
It can get no better than this
And if the world was to end tomorrow

There'd be no more time I could borrow
So I guess right now today
I'll love her until I'm weak, or until my breath
has faded away...

When it comes to love

When we touch

I'll be off work in about an hour
And come see you the very second
I'm out the shower
I've been anticipating seeing you
Smelling good feeling good
You're just something I can't get off my mind
So all day I've actually been writing you to the
pages to complete my story
So I gotta get a little bit closer
I'll be there less than an hour
Besides
I got tomorrow off
So I'm planning on an all nighter with you
So I'm standing off
I can go for steak
But I know you want the lobster
And for dessert you can have the nectar
And you know I'm at you like the Cookie
Monster, we gonna get this better
Oh yeah love, you gonna get this work
And afterwards we just might need church
Due to the things that's bound to go down before
the night's over
It's been awhile since we dated and that's
something we don't want to lose

We gonna get it crackin, and I guarantee the
love we're going to be making is going to make
the news
I'm so excited
Just thinking about you in this shower has got
me feeling some type of way
And I'm not with touching myself
I'm a let you do that for me
Look, I've been saving myself for awhile
Just to explode on you when running wild
Love, this is how the story go
It's a milky flow leaving you soggy like a
dipped Oreo
Love, you do something to me
I'm so out of it
I just want to be the chocolate chip in your cookie
Lady I'm filled with fruit so just taste me
Can we make a love scene?
Make our own steam
Fill you up instantly to watch it run over like
melted cookies and cream
Dream me daily
I'm almost there
So just meet me on the stairs with the doors
unlocked in your boy shorts, I don't want your
average underwear
Black boy shorts on and a hair tie
Hoop earrings

Pretty fingernails, oil rubbed halfway into your
thighs, me in your eyes
And a few bath towels on the bed
Naaaaaahh, no sheets just a mattress
And a few shots of Patron
And fan with some ice instead
And some beautiful neck bone
Trust me love, I can stay strong
Playing with your imagination
Cookies and cream
Crushed in ice cream
I moan, you scream
I'm still a little damp, and pours open from this
shower
She knows what it is
Ain't no running
Bite down on this for about a half an hour
Then the cycle can start over
When we touch it's always sweet and never sour.

With you

With you it's like I have no conscience about
what I do as long as I'm with you, it doesn't
matter, love is so true when we're through

Knowing we're dead wrong

Asking one another how was it, after we put our
cloth back on, and head home

I was this close to grabbing you in lane 7 at the
market the second he turned his back

Yeah, I caught you looking back

I can see it in your face, you felt you was out of
place, but love don't make mistakes

You was just caught in a distraction

Money threw us off including busting up
headboards and burning up mattresses

Hit me up when you get home

Try not to stare at this for too long

Send me a picture when you get to the car

I'm lost for words

Just last night we was all laid up

And he didn't even notice you came home
smelling like that Usher with dried up run off
smeared up make-up

He don't notice you like I do or like I did

If home is where you want to be,

that's where you'd be

But if you want to be here with me

Here is where I sleep

We don't have to creep to eat

This can be an eternal feast

Just you and me

A private party daily here at our home

this can be us

All you have to do is give me the word

We were lovers before you plug into it with him

So stop playing with him and come home

I can only wait for so long

Before your pillow is replaced

I will always love you, but if that's where your mind is, give him your heart too

And quit leaving it in the bed with me

Pick and choose somewhere

I don't want you to see me with another and be feeling some type of way, when I already given you the opportunity

To live life with me

But you didn't want to do me

You just wanted to do me

And it was more to me then what you taste

Black Coffee

Black Skin

I'm your shadow in the sun, the star standing next to your moon, the Hershey in your kiss, the wave in your Nile, your dew in your mist,

Black skin

You're the Queen of the earth, God's gift at birth

I don't know what it is, I am flowers, I am candy, I am whatever it is you're worth

You're worth more than any diamond found in a mine; a jewel undiscovered before it's time

The sun envies you

Black skin ......

I'm dying to get in

The hidden treasure to my seed

The reason that I breathe, you're the butterflies in my stomach, a dream that means so much to me

I see you I need you I want you I bleed you

I love you ...

Black skin

You are the most gorgeous thing God created in his image

How could we ever let you down?

And create such damage

The average couldn't handle you

It a take a king to run this through

Black skin, African Hebrew

You're priceless

When can I see you?

I want to get to know you

I know it may seem odd

but looking into your eyes, I know I seen a God

He molded you with his own hands, so all glory goes to him

The creator of the heavens and land, oh goodness Lord forgive me for my sins, because the thoughts I have of you sends goosebumps down my black skin

I admire you and got love for you in...

Your black skin

Dose of Medicine

There isn't any other way that I would prefer to have you

It's more than sex or a complex

Or text

I respect your dominance, your common sense, so just check you...

Your insecurity shouldn't exist

My soul is placed in your abundance

These outsiders mean nothing, it's irrelevant

When I'm in you it's like I'm out of space with no gravitation

Just the stars and the Milky Way, and if there were any other place I'd rather be, it would be in the eye of your soul, or you sleeping on my face

Where it's warm and never cold, recognize what is love and not a mistake

Rest.... you no longer have to drift

Allow me to finesse and bless and overflow
within you all that's empty

God has given me you, and in you I have given
me

Don't flush time away

Or you'll regret remembering the first day

Push and I'll push back

Then tell me if you like that.... whisper into my
ear that hush sound

Like shhhhhhhhhhh just like that

Stay right there don't move, because that's it

Just push and I'll push back, just squeeze me
tighter

All rain and no spit

As we lock the doors of heaven

And put out hell with lose lips

This is an explosion, at the same time birthing
new love

With a lower kiss

Push and I'll push back, I'm not going nowhere
I'm right here just (bite that)

The doors are locked outside so there's no need to
worry, no one's coming in every part of you is
all me

You're my only fetish

I'm starving

I crave only you till the end

I am part of you

Now feed me you

you're my dose of medicine within

Unforgettable Touch

Sometimes I hope you're thinking of me

Staring at your picture still brings back memories

I'm losing control over all my thoughts

Thinking about you doing what you used to do to me, to him, and even some of the things I taught

Baby do you think about me when you're laying next to him?

Do your eyes still open and your lips form my name when your calling out to him?

Make no mistakes

You know I'm similar to an earthquake

Due to the way I used to make your body shake

I don't want to be petty

And ask no questions

But I can tell I'm not forgotten, my touch was a blessing

Pillow Talk

You can't even stand to hear my voice

But being away I guess was a better choice

So you say I was something that made you weak?

Bet you can still smell my cologne on your sheets

That Curve or that Gucci guilty

Don't play me stupid

Because I can still feel you in me

You smiling whenever I say something sweet

You biting your lip whenever I say…. you ready?

And bring that honey over to me

I got something good to eat

So you say you don't like pineapple

Well try this strawberry kiwi treat

Can I bite down on the back of your neck?

Nibble on your thighs

Spell my name on your lower back…come on love
I don't mean no disrespect

Let's let the pillow talk

While listening to you screaming

through the pillowcase

Don't bury your face because I can barely

See you in this dark due to the dim lights

Circled around your bedroom

I'm glad the fire from the fireplace has went out
because I got a little bit hot

And I see your curls fell too

Do you think about me when your laying next to
him?

Crying next to him

Dying next to him

Knowing that I am the only one who has ever
breathed life into you....

I can be a little petty

But so what, I know you like it

Hands off of you

I'm not trying to stare at you, at least that's what I was thinking, oh God if you could have only imagined what I was thinking, at that very moment when I first met you

It was crazy, I saw you sitting up here just like the way you are now, me taking you home laying you down, but wait hold up, let me just stop before I get carried away

Because I can feel the people around us are reading my lips, but at the same time staring at your hips, and I don't want to get jealous

Because you're not mine yet, at least that's what I was thinking, but my mission was to make you mine, don't look at me like that because I'm not crazy, I just know what I want so I hope your insides match your putter appearance

Man oh man, my thoughts play like a movie whenever it comes to you

I just love the way that you move me

You make all things come true

But I could never imagine us together like right now

Sipping on wine having a good time, you kicking and biting your lips

We drifting the time

Can I take your picture?

Of your figure, Lord you're so soft you're like a hot December

God's angel that I want in every angle

And in every way from the finger to the choke, to the hair pulling and wrapped around your throat,

can I bite you there, squeeze you there, in many places only God knows

Can we make it right? I'll make you my wife, and not for one night

But for eternity...you give me insight, you bring out the best in me, I was trying not to look, that's what I thought when I first laid eyes on you

But I got you now

And I can't seem to take my hands off of you

I remember you

She stared at me as she stepped out of the truck
as she caught my eye taking a quick look

"I see you looking" as she replied, even though I
wanted to lie and say, no I wasn't, I responded
and said, "don't I know you?"

She smiled and said, "oh that was slick"

With her cherry red lip stick on looking so thick

She responded, "I'm more than this

More than what you see

You going to speak? Or are you going to
continue looking, staring breathless at me?"

"Lady someone like you has got to have a man
under the bush somewhere" I said,

She laughed in response saying, "no there isn't,
because all I attract is low lifes and I'm beyond
that, so what's good with you?

Is that your comeback?"

I said, "I've haven't came yet"

Then I told her my name

She told me her name was Diana

And she had that candy rain

"Oh, you got jokes" I replied,

"No, I just know what attracted you" she says,

"Well baby I'm not like other guys and I see way beyond the bed" I said

"Yes, I like to have fun

But with you I see a little bit more

So can I get your number and keep you in store?"

"oooweee look at you" is all she could say

Two weeks went by lady called me and all she had to say

Was...." come and get me

I'm in need of company

Come and scoop me

I know you crave to touch me"

It was at that very moment I knew what was up

I jumped into my truck

And 15 minutes later I pulled up

Looking into her eyes had me mesmerized

I put my hand on her thighs

She's that which caught me by surprise

She leaned over to kiss me, I tried my hardest not to lose grip, as I spin my wip

She bit my bottom lip

Which caused me to pull over

To grip her hip

Lost at a truck stop, things got heated

As the rain drops, we were both soaked and wet with drenched cloths

Wearing flip flops

She wanted it right then and now

But I thought what if the police came?

It was the thrill of the moment

Then I walked into her heatwave

Deep breath gasping

This was on another level

I was shook, but feeling good

And couldn't stop, I turned into the devil

She pulled something out of me

As the lights from the other cars hit the bush

I closed my eyes and begin to focus, not taking
another look

We were like animals in the wild

This woman was unreal

All that bounce

Made me crave jello

I was like Superman hard as steel

And when it was over, she took a sucker from out
her purse, which was a sour Carmel apple

So seductive with her green lips

That taste so sweet, I went in for seconds

Like, "can I touch you?

at least one more time before I drop you off?" and
she smiled, Round 2 and said,

"come in boy, let me set you off"

We were now in the back of the pickup

She giving me all sorts of knowledge

When the people on the road passed, it was as if the truck had hydraulics

Pretty little lover

She was something I'll never forget

This was the quickest little dive

That I love, I'll never really ever forget

I remember you so....

I'm not afraid

When I was younger, I used to be afraid of
women like you, because I used to think that you
were too much

But the very second I got a sample of that honey I
couldn't resist its touch

To me we might be compatible

But better yet you might be light weight

And edible

Me and you together, I can see it

we might be something incredible

you're food to my soul, you stimulate my mind
without physically touching my grind

you're my hunger and my thirst

Your loves shoots beyond paradise, it creates a
new universe

Hey pretty lady, here's my heart in exchange for
yours

I love your rolls and stretch marks and pretty
dimples on your booty

I pray we never grow apart

Your short or long hair

 added on with the cinnamon scent you leave
gracefully in the air

I love the pretty faces you make just by me
rubbing your feet

And the pineapple taste she gives me, that taste
like skittles when I'm down to feast

You're so good to eat

Baby you're so good to me

You make my life complete

I'm drowning in your dreams before I fall to sleep

My African Queen, my big beautiful blue
butterfly bumble bee

Loving your sweet buttermilk biscuit

Covered with honey

You're something like no other

Sharing you is impossible, so tonight I'll give
birth in you, my appetite, I'm savage

And also greedy

You do just that to me

Bring out the poetry in me

I envy the sheets I spill on because my ink

Most times are sticky

I'm not afraid of you no more

Please king me

She brings butterflies to my stomach

Time and time again when people see me with her, they say, oh my God, and I say, oh yeah

My baby is a whole lot of woman

She so soft and everyday tempting

That's why I'm with her

She eases my mind and daily she's pleasing, she feeds me and teases me

Can't nobody take her or make her

She's sweeter than a gummy life savor

Oh God whenever I break her

She follows up and returns the favor

Gives me hi-fives

She's so live, she's something that I love to cater

I could never hate her

Just look at her

She's soul food to my soul

She's my cabbage, crushed, soaked up In cornbread

Finger licking country fed love

She's something like a fine red wine

Served with the sweetest peach cobbler

Baby love lobster

Even though I don't even bother

But I don't get down with all that taste testing

She's my favorite, which is my cranberry and duck dressing

She's a whole meal

The real deal for real

What you gotta say?

She gives more than face, she got brains

She's German chocolate

My candy rain

She gives me the munchies

Baby's that white widow strain

I get high mentioning her name

And it's a damn shame that her love hits me like dope in a plate

And that's something I hate

Because when I can't get her

I feel trapped mentally and can't escape

"Can I get seconds?" Is what I ask, then she says "boy go on ahead and help yourself

This food right here is going to always last"

My baby is a whole lot of woman

Getting a whole lot of me

This plate right here is for free

Yes, indeed fit only for a king

King me

Ooweeeee...

You're a dream, spoken into reality
Ohh baby,
You're the best part of life,
Beauty's fatality

Love,
When I first saw you,
I just knew I had to have you
Face you, taste you,
Every piece and part of you

I had to make you mine
My backbone blown,
On top of cloud nine
I'm so proud
With the widest smile,
Your style,

Just breaks me down

Okay, I can actually say your mine
Fine wine and one of a kind
Far from a Barbie,
You feed me
When I starve, see

Ohhh so classy, sassy,
with a nice firm Backside
I.... See,
You know what I like...know what I love,
I want to be the bubbles in your tub,
The wet sheets when we make love,
The lip that is softly bitten,
When you say you can't get enough

Ohh baby excuse my French,
I just can't wait until we get home

Ooweee,

Am I really your husband?

I'm loving this,

Blended with your sexy tone

Smelling like Beyoncé,

And it's crazy,

Because I got on Jay Z gold

You make my imagination run wild

I just can't wait till we get home

Just to squeeze your feet and caress your thighs,

Look in your eyes,

Like, oh my God!

Real Woman

I love how she turns heads as she walks by...and
she's all mine

And I love how she's a river that never runs
dry...and that's my soul tie

She's my fire in my secret place

 My lover, my desire in God's Grace

Lord, she's all woman

Built and made from the dust especially for me

She's my sugar in my yams

The beauty in any rose

The last breath that I take in a climax

That itch that I scratch whenever I need that,
she's all mine

And I'm a show her off to the world

I get goosebumps whenever she touches me, it's
like my body freezes and curls

She's my Juice Box

And I'm her gravy on her dressing, and together
we make the sweetest sauce

 When stirred

She turns heads, look at her

there isn't nothing like my baby

She's German chocolate

And can touch on every topic

She got brains and a lot of booty

No, I'll never keep a secret from her

Because she has that honey love

That drives me crazy

Can we go half on a baby?

Because your love is one in a million

 That I know if I ever lost it

It a take God for me to find it again

I'd die without you

Can I touch her nice and slow?

Like Usher?

I'll be gentle just a little

But I'm a lover of her

Lord my baby turns heads

Just look at her

Many want to call her fat

But I prefer thick because I like them like that

Look at her crown she holds down

Queen is written all over her

There isn't none like her she is original

See

ain't no Nikki or Cardi B image compared to this queen

Barbie where?

That's what I thought, this is a real woman

Now watch my baby turn heads

She's more than anything I've ever had

She's more than anything that I've ever had
More than a dream or an illusion
Standing on a bridge in the blazing heat
because I can touch her
I can feel her...they say love like this doesn't
really exist
Then why is she existing in front of me?
My queen...
If the world only knew all the things I've been
through to get to you
She knows what buttons to push
And what keys to play
Words to say with a voice that prays
I can stand to be alone
Because I'll always have you mentally even if
you're not near me
But whenever you're close
You're not only next to me, but inside me
We are becoming one......
No one compares to you
Those stressful heartbreaks made me better for
you

It created me into the man and taught and
showed me love
So I thank my past
For molding me into my great so I can receive
My greater
I am so ready for you
We are becoming one...
So many tears for years and wasted time
I stroke my last stroke
And suck my last soul
Out of its shell
Giving all of me into something that can't even
see its own worth, will never happen again
You are becoming my only best friend
The journey is over
There's no more searching
No more crazy questions of insecurities
Because you now have all of me and I have all of
you
We are becoming one....
She loves me not because what she can gain from
me
But what she can maintain and build and feel
from one another
We don't only look good together
But we feel good together

We are the perfect match inside out
Another me, never...
Another her...there can never be better
She's God's gift
Ready for me to unwrap her
She's my new
My honey dripping from the moon
We are becoming one

Signing me away

Baby when I said it was all good

That's exactly what I meant

Me and God came together, and I accepted it

I signed this covenant with him to become one with you

My love is God

And God is my love

And through him I know I'll be perfect for you

You are my soulmate

The love I've waited for day by day

For years I sat patiently waiting, seeking, then finding, defying all my timing,

Correcting my flaws for any cause, just to line up with you

There isn't too many like you, so God had to put together the perfect match

You are the fruit in the garden

That can be purposely eaten, that I will attach

I sign all of me over to you

As you sign all of yourself over to me

Now we are one

So juicy, so sweet, so ripe from Gods tree

I am the key to your juice Box

You are like the pressure crushing all my past in the deepest ocean

Can I be the lava in your volcano?

That flows like a river, just say so

I'll do anything you want and be everything that you need

I want to be your deepest sweetest dream

I'm down for only your team

Can I kiss your face?

In every way

Can I lick your lips just to taste your grace?

Let us sign with the pen of God right here

On our hearts

Let our souls dance to a tune that never departs

Let us die together

Knowing God is in us

Let no one come between us or stand against us

Be my shield and I'll be your sword

I want to make you feel

Like you're overdosing on me more and more

I'm signing me away

I am becoming more than your man

I am becoming your King to a wife

From the brown sands

My queen

Is what you'll be

You'll see, just trust me

Sign right here on this dotted line

And I guarantee

I'll make it well worth your lifetime

value me now

If you would only let go.... life would be fair to you

And let someone love and take care of you

Many want what is fun until reality hits them, until their soul is numb

They throw away their good and in the end regret life due to what was

Misunderstood

Cherish what you have, or someone will show you

Love what you've thrown away

Your blessings will go astray

And flashbacks will taunt you like, wow

All you have is memories

Choose wisely

With what you have

Or leave what's good alone

Or feel the wrath

Let someone else have and cherish what you thought you wanted

Let them live and move off on it

Let them be that wife or husband

That lover that you weren't

And love what you've always wanted, which possibly was nothing

Your lover should be your best friend

And not no other

I guess this is the life we live so why even bother?

Love which is something a lot of people will never understand,

until it's gone

and when that one we didn't really appreciate started him or her a new life

When that special person makes them forget all that strife

When there's no longer bandages on the heart or stitches,

but he or she has given

them something that makes their heart feel
brand new right from the start

Things happen for a reason

Like great lessons learned

Love can be temporary

Especially to those who left your heart to burn

Cherish love and life now, while you have it in
your presence

My friend

Where have you been

Where have you been my whole life?

Maybe you were always there just

Waiting for me to get things right

I've been through a few lovers, but most
definitely I know not like you

None couldn't even compare because the love you
give is so true

Your thighs and your mind are so divine

Come on baby tell me

Just what would it take to make you a lifetime of
mine?

You just don't know how I would change this
very life for you, would never be the same

I've had my ups and downs

But never really fooled around

I was saving my heart just for you

And I think it's time I held you down

I'm not like the other lovers you've once had before, just let me in

I know you hear me knocking at heaven's door

Sex can wait, this is fate

Let the haters hate

We can escape

I'll make you shake, don't drop no weight

I want all of you from the pie to the cake

Flood your river to a lake

Disfigure your face

With the love I make

I want you ugly biting your lip

Don't you got something for me? Just wiggle your hips

I'm feeling your wave, just take me away

Don't hesitate

When backboards break

Just keep on moving and I'll keep on soothing

We'll find our wings

To fly into our movement

Yes, where have you been all my life?

I think it's time I make you my wife

Will I ever Find

Will I ever find another lover like you? Is what I ask myself

Another woman so true. I always ask myself

Will I ever find another that made me feel so brand new like you? Lost in the wind over you, seasick, feeling blue

Wishing you would catch my tears

Wishing I had you near to love you a thousand years

Good morning beautiful, last night I really felt your beautiful love

Good morning beautiful, is how I used to make her feel, to get her day started with a simple touch...

I could remember when she used to lay on my chest and grab me

taste me

on her lips that drove me crazy

I was good for thought, but her heart was in a maze, see.

she was confused

 used to the mental abuse

 all it took was for this pathetic nigga to say was "sick baby he doesn't deserve you"

so...16 years

Of friendship gone down the drain

Love started to evaporate like rain

And she told me it was complicated

With a direct cold stare my tire gave in, and she was right there, man oh man I had a girl filled with pain

Whose life was not fair

But in a short period of time she had me pulling on her hair

taking off her clothes

Love was not aware

Damn I had a girl, one you would dream about

You wouldn't believe I loved

I feel I can't breathe without, I fiend about

Her touch

The moves she made was like 20 years we laid

how could she bury us and fade?

I dread the love we made; I wish I never touched
her to this day

Somebody give me an answer

 this love is on me like cancer

Everything I do it reminds me

wishing she come through and just rescue me

I'm in a chain, I need prayer, it has bound me

Love I thought wouldn't have drowned me

I can still feel you baby and it's crazy

Because I had a girl...

I had a girl...I had a girl

Sitting, chilling at work zone all by myself

My heart is with you, but my mind is with
someone else

And it's not fair to the one who loves me

Because my soul has a fetish for you

Love is stubborn and I can't help but think of you

But I'll get over it through time, but right now

What's a grown man supposed to do?

Look, I still taste you on my lips

And it's a trip, what am I to do?

With your scent on my sheets, I still smell your sweet perfume

I had a girl who was the jack of all trades

Who felt the love that I made

Who kept me deep in her, I slept in her

I... I had a girl

I had a girl...I had a girl....

That was not of this world

She was the closest I got to perfect

Wine I Love

You are exactly what I paint in perfect words

A goddess dropped out of the galaxies

And worships the God I serve

The perfect wine I swallow down that relaxes my soul

my hot and my cold

that causes my heart to unfold

When I praise, you are already in the gates

When I cry out, you're already seeking Gods face

You are the perfect taste, the grace of melon so sweet

I fall to my knees every night thanking and asking God why is he so good to me? for giving you to me

So sassy and with class

You can be a freak when it's time to

But people could never guess

That part of you, I bring out of you, you give to me

And yes, I love to show you off

You're nowhere insecure

Or jealous, and even at times I set you off

You're not petty and don't dig into my past

To use broken pieces as weapons to trigger me

You communicate, which is a big turn on

You're so relaxed when you correct me

I have no pride baby, whenever it comes to you

I'll give you my time cause you always stay true

You never hold in a situation

We talk it out and all the way through

You're the perfect wine I stay drunk off

only if it's you

You give me my time and when I return home

You still treat (it)

Brand new

A virtuous woman is what you are

I'll bare my seeds through

Straight from the heart

Your thighs, eyes, hair and stare is what I like

But it's your mind that I love that keeps me high

The perfect wine I love

My Sinful Obsession

Beautiful

Sitting here thinking like damn

All that loving for nothing, so all you have to
say is sorry and that it wasn't your intentions

To walk back through a closed door

What for? You're not going to even hear me out

Block out my calls, so this is what we do?

He shed a couple of tears and proposed to you,
toss a few bottles in the air

Threaten to kill himself if you wouldn't come
back, watch your house post up

Which caused you to look back

I'm bugging, all this good loving pissed out like
alcohol, when I was there to catch you when you
fall, I was everything he wasn't

This is what we do?

You bounce on me a few times and taste this
sweet wine

Yeah, it's freaked up

The situation is all blown up

But how can I get mad because relocating from another, I threw everything away just to make face,

And you still turned away

Well I hope he's loving you like I did

But that's impossible

Because you know deep down inside that there can only be one me

And I know you still feel me deep

I was that door that opened and shut for you

That first voice you heard every morning that said, damn your beautiful

But this is what we do

Throw things away

I would of never done half the things he's done that pushed you away

I'm too old for play

I'm a real man ,something I guess you'll never understand, because love is dysfunctional on your end, and is more than a meaning itself to me, it's more than the cars and clothes I've bought, the trips we took or even the house we sought

The blueprint you folded up and threw it away, I'm praying he doesn't leave you or cheat on you for the sheep he's dissed you for in the past

I'm praying the bottle doesn't overtake the love he has for you and that it last

Because I'm original and you know I'm something you've always dreamed, that you possibly wasn't ready for at all

You were in love with the thought of loving me

Your bounce was something like a drug to me

But my stroke will forever be an infection

Through your walls finessing you

In every direction

Just the thought of me

And that first night I made your reality a dream

Just pray to God we're not zoned off one another at the same time, you making love and you scream out my name

My love is like voodoo

I'm in you like a screw loose

Squeezing you loose like a fruit juice

You will remember me

Beautiful

Behind her smile

Behind her smile was a broken heart

She carried warm tears that feared she'd fall apart....Sweet like cake but freshly baked...

Who would of ever thought she'd fade away in just a day.....searching for love she couldn't find but love found her, but yet she was blind...heart scarred from a dead past praying that love got better, she turned her head to go left thinking like Keith Sweat, hoping it last forever, this cycle had me gripping my Bible

Lost due to me carrying a title

God said let it go or pick up a rival

The mind is weak and that I must bypass this situation, this love was seasonal, let it go

Smiles and tears and actions of illusional years

There's no such thing as perfect

But pain of closure and tears

One last kiss before I close the door

She covered her face as the tears fell to the floor

Here's your key to the car and the rings you gave to me,

But can I have back that small piece of my heart? yeah that piece called the memory

I can still taste the chili and the nacho dip out the bowl, isn't that crazy?

How a person can tie to you crying, saying they love you, and you're loving them as if you're trying to make a baby, life living is crazy....

And they don't look back and not have a care in the world

They have a drink to numb their heart, and say f...it here's to a new world

A smile and a stare and one gaze into the eyes

Can cause rain to fall

Like a tsunami between your little thick thighs

She knew what it was, and will always remember how I made her rain fall

Like me having her running with her face buried in the pillow, by the fireplace with my love like a thermometer taking her temperature

Baby cakes small fingers

Slanted eyes sweet as Zingers

But behind her eyes there were tears dying to fall, and soon released Full with a past of the streets, hard to forgive she stayed sleep

A lost jewel and angel with wings looking up

Afraid to touch the clouds

Because of love that doesn't possibly love her

Baby's more valuable

Than what she can and could imagine

She's magic in the right hands

A wife to the right man

But behind her smile

There's pain she refuses to let go

So she works herself like crazy

to ease her soul.... a painful smile but a beautiful cry

I've seen all this in her eyes

But once I noticed it, she turned away

And my heart said I told you so

She cried that I wouldn't leave

But her heart was confused like yoooo!

My spirit said love isn't complicated

She's confused so let it go

I smiled and said she'll be alright, gave her a tear and closed the car door

And gave her back the life she was used to

And comfortable with

And that's when she realized that's what she wanted anyway...

Beautiful broken smile

Kissing her cheeks drove me wild

It's just too bad

Love was limited to and thrown back to a past

Like a lost file

Another lost angel that none of us who really deserves to see

And a real man will never get a chance to keep.

Borrowed Time

I ask myself what am I doing here with you,
It's morning...and you're still laying here with
me? I think that I am falling
In love with you, but it's not good for you and
me...
I'm tempted to call in because of that thing that
you do to me
Girl, you gonna have me stalking
Calling off for the rest of the week
I'm watching you sleep in
While your phone buzz off knowing

that it is him
I know he feels all the love that you're giving to
me, but it's no proof that you're with me baby,
this is crazy
We were only supposed to be friends
So why do I feel like I want to be your man?
As you talk about my eyes, telling me how
much you've been wanting to ask me can you
kiss me,

it's funny
It's funny how a kiss got us in a situation like
this, You stealing the covers or balled up close

under me
I can feel your breath on my chest
While my chin rest on the top of your head
And I'm clutching you close down on your
breast
I can't believe you're still laying here
with me
Last night I was in a heavy mood
Ready to explode
You're here with me because he was never on that
heat I'm on
Lost in these sheets
Where do we go from here?
When I'm not supposed to be here
When we are not supposed to be here
We both were in need of one another
He wasn't bringing you that fire
And she wasn't getting me no higher
This is borrowed time
I've seen you staring, trying so hard not to
You wanting to speak so bad
But he was somewhere near watching you,
watching me
Now I'm staring at you laying on my pillow
Thinking in the next moment you got to wake
up and leave

Knowing my position
You feeling guilty creeping and

sleeping with me
We can't keep doing this
That's what you would say right after we finish
But you wouldn't tell me to stop
We would take one deep breath and hit the square
And jump right into it
Like we didn't care...I got you here with me
And I can't believe it
This is borrowed time
And I crave the taste of it

I don't cross your mind

If only you let me...

Be that reason and meaning due to the sweet
taste of sweet wine in love with the essence of
your crave for the Jamaican me Happy

Late nights twisted, and I know you be missing
my love and my kisses

Ooooweeee pretty smile don't stay gone

It ain't the same like it is or what it was with me
I see...he ain't opening up car doors for you baby
tonguing you like crazy up out of your sleep

I'm deadly love

And you know it when it comes to me

Let me remind you as I position myself behind
you...pulling your hair while smoking a square

I see we're almost out of'em

Hold up let me kiss you right there

Has he told you?

You were beautiful today

If not, well let me be the first

I thirst for your waterfall on my thighs

And watching your eyes roll back into your mind

Oweeeeee this love is crazy, it's almost like it's make believe, I'm that new strain of weed you need to cure your need

You can't say you're happy baby, don't lie to me

Vanilla flavored now and later

Gummy bear tasting life savor

I can see the smile emerging on your face now

But I'll respect you how...?

By loving you down mentally until you come back around to lay down with a king

This right here is more than sex

It's a mental complex

Shhhh just let me bury my face into your neck

And blow and suck and lick on your brown skin and get in where I fit in... could you

Pour me another glass would you please?

Hmmmm, I love the smell of your perfume

As I stand behind you drift through the breeze

With your sexy red lingerie

Baby please pose for me ...walk around love, keep the lights dim and walk over slow to me

Take it off and toss it to the side of the left side of the bed

Let love kiss your lips with the sweetest taste

Now place my love inside and love him...

What was alive let's keep it dead

Then resurrect us with no towels on the bed

Wets spots on each corner

Bite down on the pillow cause now I own her...

You'll forever remember me because in your mind that loving will always be mine

Until you detox me out of you

And that's possibly impossible

Because your apart of me

Which is why you sleep in silence

It a never be the same because I'm forever right there

It a never be the same because in your mind you'll always compare

It a hurt you to see me in public

Due to it a make you wonder like, oh my God

I wonder who's getting all his good loving

Picturing if and what I'm doing to the next

Oh God, is he flipping and loving her at his best

Missing me, loving me baby, and you know he ain't me

Cause I love crazy

I love as if we're planning a baby

Yeah, I bet …heck naw I know …. it's driving you crazy

And you can't say I don't cross your mind….

Dysfunctional Love

You wouldn't believe it if I told you I had a
woman who told me she loved me within two
days

Spent the night with me practically the first day
the connection was crazy

A different type of Lady

She fed my mental and sexuality was amazing

But it was a catch which made us a perfect match

We both had been broken but something told me
don't be so quick to attach

We exchanged keys to her wip

and her debit

It was a trip

she catered to me like a king served me breakfast

We zoned off her dangerous lips

When it came to the grooving, I was proving

Never to ask

she knew exactly what I wanted and needed

I Jumped on her fast

 but it was too good to be true

Something gotta be wrong

Singing her songs, waking up in cold wet spots

From loving her all night long

What's wrong? Is what I would ask her catching her daydreaming off, "I gotta ex-boyfriend that seems to not want to take off

He watches my house and watches your media live, he knows your fb page

And that shhh is on my mind "

He had her heart and I had her mind, but I was like yo, maybe it's almost time for me to give her up, especially she telling how complicated things were now

I bugged out like wow, this woman has introduced me to half her family, bought wedding rings, planned on marrying me too etc.

It was crazy just to call me back in the next 2 days to tell me sorry, I don't want you to get hurt and how gangsta this dude was

Pillow Talk

Ricky this was not my intentions everything
was real and especially my love

I smiled and said, you good

Kissed her deep and before I closed her car door

she buried her face, cried her tears on to the car
floor, then text me and said, it's life that's what
dating's all about

Which is the weirdest type of dating I've ever been
involved in, ouch

She freaked and tasted me as if we were married

I swallowed her soul to the point my love making
moved objects around her room, as if I possessed
the powers of Carrie

Scary, please understand me

If she say she don't think about me

It a be a natural lie, and that's scary

She got a part of me she possibly shouldn't have
gotten

Now she's going to be looking for me in him

Until her soul has rotten

She should have just left real love alone

And stuck to the counterfeited

She should have just liked or loved a picture

And continue to love what she was used to

Dysfunctional love

Because I'm abnormal, my type of love put her out of place

Which explained a lot, hmmmmmm

For this Moment

Sometimes I wish my heart was similar to yours,
I wish I had a heart that shared no regret and
that could easily walk away from things
without a care in the World

A heart that says I love you, but at the same time
wouldn't think twice about walking out of your
life, I guess I'll just have to seize the moment and
love you while I can before you take your stand,
Yes, I guess I understand I really have no choice

Due to the mind of man

Loving you as much as I can

I'm afraid to love another

Because with you I've done the best I can

Making love to you with my soul

Like no other man

I don't try to be different, but I am in this dying
land

I wish I had a heart like yours, but I guess God
gave me his

I can't just turn my back on what I say I love
like I don't care

That type of love is deception still

Love never hides or lies but gives....

Compassion

It caters, it prays, it shines, it lives

I guess I'll love you for the moment

Until your mind says enough

Because your heart only speaks it seems like
when things get tough

I guess I'll love you for the moment

Because eternity you can't see

I thought it was forever

Or until the death of you or me

Covered under grace we bonded in his face

But you broke it for these streets!!

You looked back and became salt

And I was Lot

Faithful, willing, but I walked

I wish my heart was like yours, with not a care in the world

Loving with no ties

Running with lust, lies, with dry eyes

Holding in pain

That's molding my image damaging my sanity

Blocking Gods vision

I wish I had your heart

Because I love too hard and you love soft

Which explains why love like yours is so easy to cut and turn off

I wish I had your heart

But God gave me his

So I guess I'll just love you for this moment all while I can

Ricky Boone

I Could Have Fought for Her

I could of fought for her

But she also had to want love for herself

Why sit around like a sad sop feeling like baby, why don't you want me anymore...?

Fine, go ahead leave

And watch my soul bleed

Due to you'll eventually dream and spirit scream for me because

One day his love will fade out on you, because it's not the love you seek

No baby I'm not pressed

But I was a bit stressed

Because I knew I could of been done better than you, but hey you was cute

And I just wanted to get to know you

But ended up sleeping inside you

Breakfast in bed

Breakfast was head

Pillow Talk

We were wilding out late nights spending bread

Wine and good open conversation

We both could follow

Making love until tomorrow

Now the memories similar to a sorrow

I wanted to pick up the pieces

to all the things he did

Your mind needed to rewind

You were so sweet when I first met you, but
listening to your family members left things
cold as heck in late December

I'm so much different

I just paid close attention

I'll never cheat I've never made you cry

All I needed you to do was follow me

I wanted to spend my life with you

Tasting you

Touching you

Pleasing you, needing you

But you couldn't wait up for me

Like I would of waited for you

Yeah, I'm not pressed

But a bit bitter and stressed

The same plans we once made you through
shade, and merged it to the next

The moves you've made

Aren't new

This was something that you have always
been used to

But a lesson learned

And yes, it did burn, but it made a king firm

But you and I know what it is

You can tell him whatever it is you want

Mentally when you see me

You remember me

I keep you stuck in a zone

Turning you over Mentally, and I'll tell you
when it's over

Then I'll tell you when to get up

Whenever you fed up

Hopefully one day you'll see

I just wanted to love you baby

I'm a Try to Keep Myself to Myself

I'm a try to keep myself to myself
But you just send off this vibe that makes me
want to unhide the freak In me that's inside, I
can't deny
You say all we're going to do is watch a little tv
and maybe study
But in reality just to be real
I want to watch you, I want to study you
You say bible study
But your body is saying, come and touch me
You have already possibly pictured me...
You on top of me
We tasting so sweet
Tell me how you feel about it
And I'll be about it
We can make it so elite
I can read a chapter, and you can read the next
I talk the talk but I'm about mines
If you keep watching the clock
I'm a stop time
Lady what's up
I can't be touched
Get rid of ol boy, due to he's out of luck

Once the shirt comes off
I'm a throw the legs up
Like a deuce sign
Love so sick it's selfish
Crack you wide open like a shellfish
I can't help it
Yes ,the words I speak
I bring that heat
Sweep you off your feet
Yes, we shouldn't be here
But we're here
So what we gonna do?
Let's not waste time
Now can we study.....

Love for a season

The best part of you was the conversation

You taught me patience

And showed me business

You kept me close in such a short period of time

It was that season

I guess that was your definition of love

Smiles on your face wasn't enough

but you couldn't get enough

It was more than just sex with you

It was everything

You made what's was broken feel so brand new

That's what made it hard to get over you

But it was in that season

Tasting the butter cream or Carmel from off your finger from the bowl

You've done everything to please me from the depth of my soul

But it was too good to be true, it was a pain

That was always there

So I continued to be that band aid at the same time pulling on your hair

It was in that season

You gave love a meaning and

a reason to believe in

In such a short period of time

It felt like two years we were together

I almost thought we were meant to be

Because we act as if we were one another's better

Drying your tears

From crushed years

You feared to start all over

But you went back to what your heart was used to and that it couldn't get over

It was just that season

We can love someone for a season

And get the lesson and its meaning

You made me better, now I can be great

Now I value the love I have to give

While you still continue dreaming fate

I'll continue to live

You loving me and me loving you was for a season

And when you say I do

I hope you know the true meaning

Don't just turn love on and off like it's a water fountain

Or leave the sheets wet with no body to drown in

Due to karma will find you

And come knocking at your front door

And all that would be in remembrance is me

Turning the pages

Thinking...I remember when I once had a man that loved me like that

I remember I once had a man

That told me he loved me everyday

That woke me up in the mornings

With breakfast on him

I remember I had a man that sung to me and that opened up doors

And sent roses to my job

Who made me smile

And dried my tears and who showed me off and spoke of me so proud

But he was in season...

Please believe this

His love was in season

My love was in season

You taught me so well

Love is not a switch that you turn on and off

Guitar String

Can I play with your guitar string?
She says she likes to be played with like a
guitar string

Trembles when I sing

On that one-night thing

So what does that mean?

I am the melody....... marinated in her soul.

I am the riffs behind her

Walking her

Waters splashing

inside her

Climb on top of me, allow me to feel your rhythm
and blues.

Can we rock and roll, till the headboards form a
tower to devour your meteor showers?

Notes that shatter glass

From your past

This love I give is built to last

Please don't tell me to stop until I run out of gas.

Please don't tell me to stop.

I crave the essence of your Juice Box drops, that unlock the hidden doors of these unorthodox spots I got

Can we make music?

She loves it when I play her like a guitar string

And I love it when she does that little trick with her tongue, I sing

Dreams she is all of me, she is poetry

She flows like thick, sweet honey,

That sticks to my lips

Her love was meant for me.

Every night I seem to slip my grip and fall into her harmony

She and I create a tempo swing

And is now a part of me

Can I play with your guitar string?

Speaking of the Pen

She told me it was complicated

So you're in love with me, but you still love him? I just don't want you to feel suffocated

Choose wisely, because my love can't be duplicated

But violated, he has your heart, but I have your mind, true love like this is hard to find

I can't and won't fight for you

Because I don't have all of you

Baby if I can't have all of you, I figure I might as well let you go

Because there's no such thing as loving half of a heart, or half of a soul

Damn, you just turned me off like a light switch, like love is a button you push

I should of known something like this couldn't be real, I'm so glad I kept my guards but still kept it real, they say some people love is dysfunctional, meaning they don't know and

don't see what love really is, I've learned it
through life by running cold and stiff

Broken hearts have granted me with the type of
love that just isn't the ordinary love, but a gift

my tip is poison if my heart is into it

And when I speak, I mean what I say, because I
spit this thing fluid

I can prove it

she says I'm in her mind like every once in
awhile

She can't think too heavy of me due to it
wouldn't be fair to him

Because the thought of my thrust still drives her
wild

That's a soul tie yes, it's no lie

I get it so high

no matter how time flies

Love doesn't disappear over night

Love doesn't grow wings and just takes flight

my love is real and brings meaning

I can still taste her Hershey'reeses

Creaming while she's screaming

Ain't no other way to explain this

My pen so high, I have no choice but to drain this

She scrambles my brain, makes love in Rivers
that shivers the sweet taste off my sugar cane

Then she overdoses me under her sun

With the finger licking finessing my face with
my fetish, crave her little sweet honey bun

My love isn't complicated

This is why I stand still, I can't just give me
away that easy at least not all of me

I'm not easy

I've loved too many with just half a heart

There's only been a couple that a hold to my
whole heart

This right here is special

There's not too many that has entered my inner
soul and trust me once they do......

The pillow then will speak

Because this love is a gift and never complicated

Only the confused would speak these things,
cause real love they've never felt it or made it,
and through you....

You placed me at my very greatest

The meaning of

We could of been more than what you imagine
something more than magic

I'm trying to figure out what had happened,
when I saw you all I wanted to do was just grab it

I wanted to give you everything and anything
three thirty in the morning, gone off patron and
we're going in, you raining on me

and I'm swimming me

I'm feeling like I'm winning and even though
you had issues I'm a still taste it

I believe love could change anything starting by
you moaning, he ain't me, I can replace him, he
ain't me he ain't with it

He don't know I had you losing control

You should get what you deserve and that's
someone like me

Given you every drop and every ounce

Remembering on my couch on how I made your
body bounce

Pillow Talk

Ohh remembering you told me you loved me

And all the things he used to do that played you, you told me

And the promise that I made, like baby, you can trust me

I'll keep you happy

And let me be the reasons to pleasing you daily and everything he's broken I'll fix it, just love me

Your mind is saying hell naw

And heart is screaming out, you crazy

Have you been thinking about me lately?

Come feed me baby, can't you see I'm hungry?

With me you can't lose

I promise I don't play when it comes to my food, I'll clean plate that a put you to sleep

On the ooze.... button

He don't have to know nothing

With me you'll have a relapse

Sounding off, I'll make your knees clap

Just take it off and squeeze it tighter (snap)

you can't handle that; can you handle that?
throw it back

I'm a pull all on your tracks

Love with me is cautious, your soul, you just
might not get that back

Baby no matter where you at

Baby sometimes I wonder

do you think about me?

When you're laying next to him, when he's sleep?

waiting for me to wake you up

Into a dream

Scream

Lady you know I care, I'm so open and going
crazy

Imagining you with him has got me tripping
lately

Because I want to love you completely due to he
can't love you like me

Girl you got me high

Thinking on how I use to and when you use to
baby, I still Love you

Baby I'm on my knees

Bleeding where my soul needs you

And I know you need me Because you've never
had anyone like me

We could of been more

Then what you've imagine

If you only knew the meaning of....

Love, It's in me

What Are We Doing?

We aren't supposed to be here

What are we doing here alone? This is crazy, who would of ever thought I'd be staring out your bedroom window

and in the next have you biting down on your pillow rolling up watching time fly

Ain't nothing in this room dry

Fan on catching a breeze as the sweat from our bodies deteriorate

Looking at each other thinking about what just took place, I can still see your face

Telling me how much you can take waiting on the next round to take place

I'm staring at the far end

Thinking where does this lead us when we are supposed to be just friends?

Now I have feelings and so do you

But you have a man, so what are we supposed to do? Venting to one another

Has got us in trouble, even though this is wrong it felt so good

And I don't want to stop this thing, it's like a drug, and I can't unplug myself from this bug that has bitten me through you

Oh God what are we doing...baby aren't we supposed to be friends ...then how are we at it again ......ooohh my

Slippery When Wet

Don't act like this is all new to you

Don't act like this is all new to you

You know how I get down

And I'm ready to go

So scoot over and let me

hop on with you

Go home with you

Baby we about to take this

here on another level

I want you spinning on me

like a Tasmanian devil

You got it made

and your body is deeper

than a grave

and I'm the shovel digging

deep off into you

don't look at me like that

You don't realize what that

look does to me, ooweee

nooo baby like that

I'll take it right here, I can't wait

I got a fetish for that Africa Taste

An all nighter til the morning

with you love would be great

Then you can brag on how

good that the love

that we make

I'm a faithful type of fellow

I'm mellow

Beating, eating your jello

Can I make it rain from the in

to the outs, no need for the

umbrella

Split you down the middle

then fill you like a cigarillo

It's about to get cold outside

Love, can we ride in?

Pillow Talk

Scoot on over, ride it slow

watch the bumps

Can I just hide in?

My tongue is foreign,

More like Spanish

My mind is chanting but

some say manish, baby I just

want you and no other I just

want you closer than lovers

Be my best friend be my rib

Be what takes be what gives

I'm Feeling those bedroom eyes

And me being between

those warm pillow soft

thighs, Baby can we leave......like

Now.

Exquisite

My taste is exquisite

She knows there isn't nobody like me, besides she loves it when I kiss it

You don't know what you're missing, my kisses aren't like no other

Now someone else is its witness

I'm exclusive

Watch her fold, can you feel it?

Make her whole, yes…I killed it

Daily and almost every night I breathe into it

I give it…… its beat

When you see her don't get mad, trust me she's now getting what you couldn't give, she's getting that good from me

But I'm letting her be great as she's getting the best of me oooweee feel

Her in deep motions

She is getting stirred like hot tea

Or honey roasting coffee

I'm her Patron blown into her hot illusion

It's hot in here, but still no confusion

We're each other's evolution

Come here love, can I kiss you there?

Feel your touch

I'm a beautiful fear

I'm not like no other

I won't take you for granted, we complete each
other

Let's get her mad...

She didn't know what she had, so we gonna let
her feel it

I'm not your average high

I'm more than a blunt, but more of an eternal
high, can I put that ....to bed

Make your body sing a Lullaby

I want to rip all of you apart

Good love making when I'm done, you'll think
that I was a porn star

Let people judge us, it's only you I'm loving

I'm what many are missing, bring me closer

I'm more than what you think

The last love couldn't handle me she got a sample

I was too real for her

I shouldn't of kept her up on the mantle

She was used to dope boys and play toys

Not barbaric kings with angelic dreams

She was only good for one thing

Bending over with loud seductive screams

But reality was a never

Can I kiss you there whenever?

Can I touch you there, can I be your brand new

More like your open care

Can we create somethings

Make a new heaven and earth

Cause we both been in hell long enough

Let us rise and do better

You're so sweet

Nothing that I've ever tasted

Your honey sweet grace, just keep bringing your
L-o-v-e my way

I want You

I don't want to ever part, it's something about you that when we make love

I don't ever want it to end, you're the best part of breakfast, I'll follow you til the end

Waking up is a thrill, I'll stand still until I feel every bit of you drown me into your open lagoon, your ocean floor overflows my greatest mood, baby move in a little closer

There's none I've ever had like you

You make me smile, and so understanding

It's so easy to take deep breaths

Oooohh whenever my eyes close, the picture moves in slow motion

Coasting every inch of me inside of you

Hmmmmm...

Baby I want you closer than ever

Can I touch your soul?

Your kiss, your tongue touching my lips

My tongue slithering around your hips, I want you to myself and no one else's

I'm yours

I want …. I want ….I want… you..

Can I have you in the morning like eggs and bacon, body shaking

Boards breaking

Have you in anyway possibly completely naked time is steady ticking

And shifting, please catch this ride

Please don't let this end

I need you to keep me inside alive

Because baby I want …I want… I want….

You….

Love like You

It doesn't rain for nothing

How do you like the view?

Lovely isn't it...we're 27 floors up, Jacuzzi tub oil body rubs, with a bowl full of strawberries and peaches, on a bear skinned rug and we'll be one

Another's drug that we dose off of

the whole nights we're here.... I'm

Something you should fear

Trust me because we're about to take this thing to a whole nother level

I'm a sit your soul outside your body so that it can catch a clear view on

What I'm about to do to you, the shrimp was good wasn't it?

It's just too bad I don t eat it, so I rock out with the rainbow trout

Dinner with fresh lemon and pepper on it...why don't you give me a second,

Let Me turn this music up a bit?

The lights are beautiful in here

I can see the gloss on your lips, Lord knows why don't you come on over here

And let me nibble on your ear...

Can we make that disappear?

I'm a take it slow

Isn't that your song baby, R Kelly tempo slow

Let me lock the door

Ooweee I'm so loving that dress

We gonna keep it on for a little bit because right now I want to fantasize you and me

At our best

The night is young

So come and get you some

Let me taste your tongue

While my body continue to embrace you while it's numb

Turn the fan on low because it's a little hot in here ohh wow baby I love the way

You smile at me

I just want to bring you near

You're like a dream come true

Eat strawberry short cake off of you

Rain on me all night, let's make a storm called hurricane YOU

Do you like the view? I knew you'd love it

Morning Dew

All of you is what I want and what I need, and
what I bleed, and what I see, and What I dream,
and what I grieve, and what I eat,
I need you more than anything
I need you in me just as well as me sleeping
deeply In you

You are my whole soul, my epitome

Life don't mean spit to me If you're not a part of
me, Lord knows you are my blessing the greatest
gift to me
Let's walk into destiny, I'd die without you
Can't breathe without you

Your thickness is my honey

I crave you like a drug I crave that rush into my
veins no joking see...
Your thighs your lips your hips I slip
into your dip
Baby please don't lose grip, because this
rollercoaster ride is not your
Average trip

I love your yams with your sweet hot water cornbread rolls

Your jalapeno pepper toes
And that punch bowl thing in the back
You look back at that bounce like jello so....
God smiles upon you like grace running from a waterfall

And when I'm down, you're always

there when I call

You're not a snack, but a full course meal

I'm full off you daily
You're so full of love that's something so real
You're not a Barbie or a rat
But classy sexy, and I love that

You know how to carry yourself as a woman

And that's a plus, so don't subtract that
So you can either pour the wine and sit back and
let it flow, and I'll go lock That front door,
And you can get dressed and be on the tips
And we can head out and I show you off

But before we leave, can I break you off?

Pillow Talk

I'm in need of that sweet black love
that turtle dove glow
those unreal Kats know nothing of

Give me all of you

And every bit of your juice
Quench my thirst with your fountains

Wake me up to that Morning dew

Ricky Boone

Orange Crush

Momma always told me as I got older that my
taste buds would change, strange because at the
age of 17 I was into the more lean queens, and
was intimidated by the thicker streams

Until I got my first taste of orange crush
She was about 255 pounds of thighs
Lower body built like a horse more like a super-
size grand prize

This wasn't even supposed to happen,
but ever since I've been hooked,
I gotta fetish for that orange crush

And she loves it when I bring that milky her
way, due to most days I crave her candy crush,
I kill her with the pop rocks overflowing with a
mint or cough drop

Giving her life filled with that cool breeze
Shattering her knees, Oh man I'm craving some
of that orange crush, baby has those cookies and
cream touch that I love so much, sweeter than
Carmel or punch bowl love

Baby sweeter than a turtle dove, I never did think
I'd even look her way, But the cake she bakes
blows me away

She's a cavity that I can stand
And if she has a man
I would advise her to lay where she stands
Because I'm bound to get a slice
And eventually the whole cake
Momma told me that my taste buds would
change

Now I love a thick thigh big breast full lip full
figure woman, that gives me range
 A woman that a give you hope and that a make
you want to change her last name

I'm craving that Orange crush so....
Oh, how I love some orange crush

Pie in the morning

Aren't you a little cold with just that sheet?

As she turns over and smiles at me

and replies "no baby, just let me get a few minutes of sleep"

As she nods her head, I respond, there's some bacon and eggs downstairs still warm whenever you ready

 "baby you cooked for me?"

She replied, "oh yeah" I said

"It's been a long night and I figure you might need a little energy from being with me

You had a deep sleep

So apparently you were weak"

she says, "boy stop, you the one who fell asleep first"

I laughed and smacked her on her butt cheek

And replied, "I don't want to eat by myself, cooked enough for us both"

She replied "baby you didn't do no toast"

"I can get that done for you, it won't take long to toast" I replied, she gets up out of bed, wraps her hair up, puts on one of my T-shirts

with some white boy shorts on

And heads downstairs and across the hallway

With each step I tread behind her, watching each ripple define her

"Lord, baby all of that is beautiful" I said,

And she replied, "thank you baby, all of you is beautiful also"

She deeply stares at me with those bedroom eyes, my mind begins to wander as my hand begins to guide and slide themselves up her thighs, she replies "aren't we going to eat?"

"Oh yeah, yeah, yes we are" I responded

As she kisses me, I begin to butter the bread

My mind is now haunted

thinking about all last night

She smiles as she waited on her toast

Pulls out the peach preserve

"This bacon is good" she says,

"You like that?" I replied, "oh yes, I see I got a man that can cook"

As we finish our breakfast and begin to chat a bit, her mind begins to drift

Like as an Usher song begins to play (can you handle it)

She comes out and says, "do you have some apple pie? Or do you want some apple pie?"

I said if it was some here of course

She said, "really? what if I told you it was a whole pie upstairs?"

And I responded, "where upstairs?"

She said, "in the bed next to the pillow

It's warm too, right next to the secret window"

I said, "give me a second, while I wash these dishes"

She headed to the bedroom

And said, "you don't know what you'll be missing, it's sweet and sour, something good and delicious"

I threw the dishes in the hot water

Started picturing me taking my T-shirt up off her

But by the time I headed to the sheets

She was already ready for me

With that apple pie already sliced

What a wife God has given to me

Dessert in the morning

I told her first to pause so I can just sit back and stare

 yeah right there

Pose in that rocking chair

Then she climbed into the bed like a black cat

Looked at me and purrrred and looked back and shook a bit

As the waves turned over her shirt

I didn't take nothing off her

She was the pie and the bed was the saucer

And my body became the fork and the knife

This was something so right

It was now morning

Born again

Ready to resurrect the night again

Can I Get a Hit?

Can I get a hit?

I just love your black and mild taste, soft skin and pretty face.

Oooh, I love when I'm at work, I just can't wait.

I anticipate, to squeeze your waste, and taste your cake

Don't hesitate, nor pull away I'm here today, all through your lake

I'll give you hope, through deep back strokes

Just lock the door and say more and more.

Can I get a hit?

Oowwwwweeee,

Our hearts beat so rapidly.

As my adrenaline rush, through each touch, I bust

Turn the music up,

I don't care,

The neighbors just going to be mad at us

Making art, throughout each and every part of
our bodies

Our souls begin to speak in different languages,

Like come inside me

Dreams of soft rivers,

Beginning to shake,

Turning into hot blizzards

You can call me the shot gun

Inhale me, as much as you can take

My wet Indian summer

Close your eyes and Imagine me like you always
do

I may be far away, but as of now, I am closer to
you

One more hit please, I beg

I need this Shot straight to the head

My pillow talks, it speaks you

This eternal life I won't ever dread

Can I get a Hit?

You know what you feel

Being with you I don't know... maybe it would seem perfect,

I would war for a woman like you and the death of it would possibly seem worth It.

You deserve more cause all I see is a heart that's soar

I wish I could give you that attention

that he's not giving you, wake you up on warm mornings tasting you

Here is a love that you've never had or felt before

It took a long time to get this skill

to feel this real

I've had a lot of broken hearts in my past, trying to work it right with the wrong ones to make it last for real

But with you I think it's possibly a jack pot situation

I could be your king and you can be my Queen and together we can create a whole

Dynasty Nation

Come here love

Have you ever been gripped up?

Secured on a high beam

I can take you to places that a have you
producing more flavors than Baskins

Robbins ice cream

You like that grip right there?

That's that love that keeps me weak

I love it right underneath that cheek, chill baby
don't worry I got you...

You got that firm grip

On that meat

I love a thick girl full figure and unique

Who stacks a pack of goodies because a king can
eat

Girl..........

But most of all I love that brain

I love a woman who can think and stay up on her
feet

You're one I could love easy

I'm that one who would run to your rescue easy
do anything you want

As long as you please and tease me

I'm a keep you right here this is your throne

And I'm not going to put you down

Until my love flows through your veins
marinating through your bones....
Do you feel me?

Zoned off of you

I'm zoned
Visions of taking you home
Turning you on with a fresh tone
Hot shower Jordan cologne rubbing your bones
Lip gloss, red wine, boy shorts, warning signs

girl you better be careful,
Gone super size
Now I'm coming live straight from behind

Now I'm a snatch your mind
Gold figure
We in a whole lot of mess
Don't stress, I'm a bless your figure
You gotta whole lot of hate, keep faith
Don't break, new man not your average trigger
Loving how your lip gloss taste,
I can tell now if it's good by the way

that you shake it
Finger licking good, said it taste like cake mix
I'm excited spark the wood, I need some patience
I hit a spot

turn the fan on because it's getting hot

in this drainage
I'm in the zone off of you
And can't get my mind off of you
But trust me, I'll manage

Give Me What I Need

A little bit of me

I can tell she's hurt
And her hearts gotten worse
She can't even recognize love if it sat in her face
and thirst for her

Being second to everything else
She tries to justify his actions
Pain is made up by a bottle and soft as a
mattress, a numb heart she says pain can't
infect her life,

she's says he doesn't respect her
I came in unexpected to give her some fresh air
Told her I was on my way in town let's grab a
bite to eat so get dressed, so do up your hair, she
said okay she didn't care
It was on

picked her up, I guess it was an old song on the
radio that took her back to when we were together,
When we really used to love one another,
It was that feeling that she couldn't find in him
it was like she wanted that old me that was
nowhere in him, but dim

I don't know what I'm going to do

She kept saying, she's been searching for love for the past 5 years and it's still slim, we had a bite to eat then headed back to my hotel for a little bit of conversation

And to freshen up, besides I had a date
And me and her was just cool, and she understood and knew that I...
Went on with my life

I went into the bathroom and showered really quick, got dressed came out she was in my bed, hold up, I thought that this was some kind of trick
I said, what are you doing?

I've seen her pain, I watched her rain, and she replied about how her life just turned crazy I spoke to her softly

And told her it a get better just sit still and take care of your babies

I walked toward the door waiting for her to put her shoes on then she looked at me seductively and said hold on...

Aye...let me show you something that you
taught me that I mastered, that I do so well...
I walked over to her due to it was something that
was drawing me to do her...

My soul right then and there begin to levitate
Marinate in her vessel's gateway
I begin to feel drained slowly and passionately
weak, She needed this

I needed this; we were both covered in pain with
nothing to lose but gain
This vulnerability chill spilled all over the hill's
mountains

She tasted life from the fountain...of youth
At that moment
She began to feel her worth
She knew love had always put her first
She knew what it was supposed to feel like being
treated as a queen

And that love isn't supposed to hurt
But make you feel like you're stuck in a
beautiful dream, and that life is what you make
it in other words make it work,
I never did make it to that date
I slept in her the whole night away

I was there to comfort and hold
An old love that I couldn't control
She sucks life out of my soul
She knew exactly what I wanted and how I
wanted it, and I gave her exactly what she been
needing

A lil bit of me...to make her feel complete
Then took her home in a full stomach
Off of a lot of me

Another 15 years

My greatest fear was finding love and losing it,
but then I found you and I valued it, smiles and
pretty kisses I took advantage of, you were
something I've treasured most I've always loved,

I waited 15 years for you and discovered you
was always here the whole time right in my city,
and that it was all on Gods time
Now I have you again at least that's what I
thought, not another 15 years will ever chance it
if losing you

I need you; I crave you, baby I'd prayed you
never leave, that's why I kept you close and
prayed endlessly

Lord bless me to bless her
Teach me to love, so that I can love her
Teach me to heal with words so that I can heal her
Let my stroke rock her boat
Coat her throat
Give her hope
let her get an understanding that we are one and
that I don't want anyone else but her
She can't be replaced

Not even til this day
I still cry for you is what I display
It's not a day that you don't cross my mind
There's not a day that the sun don't shine when I
think of you
Baby not another 15 years, I can't do
without you
I need you I so love you
Still my spirit and soul still embraces you
Not another 15 years

Can I Show You Something?

Wishing that I could show you what I picture
whenever I close my eyes

Time flies whenever you're having fun
But the sun is going down
I want some,
So I close my eyes and I begin to picture

Picture your figure on top of me
Framed in a gold frame
Drained from all the paint that I painted you in
Ooweeee, imagining me covered in you
Oh yeah, I got a little thug left in me
But I'm a gentleman first,
But still liable to give you everything you need

No need to plead
I got that antidote to make your soul bleed
But as for right now
Can I make your pillow talk to me?
Giving me all the conversation, I need if only
you believe in me.
But yet I still wonder about you!

Die In You

If I could die all over again I would and that
would be in you
Time would stop for the both of us it a be a dream
come true

I won't play with you but in you, I would enjoy
every moment of you, tell me you love me
And I'll show you how much I love you
Words don't really mean nothing if no action is
placed behind it

I can be everything you want in a man, let me
give you all my love and every minute of me I'll
give, just tell me you love me and watch me move
into action

I'm a be everything, your Lance, you be my Mia,
I'll be your best man
Your love Jones
That brown sugar that sleeps with you daily on
the phone
I want to be your dopest lyric
To a steady tempo
Dancing in your bones
I want to be that ice in your cup

That taste on your tongue that makes you crave
more of my season, your good luck...
Baby let me know...let me be the meaning
I'll make you smile even in the evening
I'm an addict that's gotta have it
A ruthless savage when it comes to my habits
I'll dig deeper then Michael Myers machete
Can I....
Baby can I ....
have my way with you?
If I could die all over again I would and that
would be in you
I see you...

Feeling Lucky

I see you finally made it

It's been a long time more like 4 years since
we've been aquatinted

Phone conversations most definitely a big
difference, it's like your tongue tied now

Can I buy you a drink?

The settings almost perfect

trust me it a be almost worth it

Once the mind begins to wander

And the body begins to crave supper, it isn't
nothing like old lovers reconnecting

You were all talk over the line

Now we're face to face and it was me you've
selected, so please let's correct this

What did you say you wanted to do once you've
gotten your hands on me?

You said you wanted to dance on me

We're not teenagers anymore

Pillow Talk

We ain't gotta lock out and sneak around baby what for?

We grown now watch out I'm a bit dangerous now at what I do

I'm a take you down into a place where lovers don't come back the same

They end up drained

merging into another lane

I'm that trip you'll end up taking, I'll be hard to shake off once I'm in your system, I'm potent like heroin, cake to a fat kid

Do things you've never did......and mention things you've never heard before spoken into your soul! Don't sip on that too fast love

It's strong but sweet

Smooth sweet like lemon tea

That's why I ordered it on the rocks

I like mine straight, but I'd rather have yours watered down a bit

Turn it down a bit

It's getting a tad bit hot

I'm feeling the way you rock the black

Your figures out cold and I can tell you gotta little fat stashed off in the back

Not too much model but brick house type

Just my type of hype

I just might...take you home if you're down to let me. You don't have to worry, I got rid of all the crazies

You funny but no dummy

Let me pay for that

Because I'm feeling lucky

Are you??

Holding Onto You

Wishing I knew exactly how you felt about me

Something about you that completes me

Nights I cry I can't sleep

Maybe we could of made love endlessly

Nights I crave you it makes me weak

This story should of never ended this way

Things I could of done wishing I could of pushed pause on then play

In my mind I'm fighting every night just to prove my love it's a battle in my mind up in here

I should of been more clear

Mindset got me feeling like a mobster

If I ever got another chance

I'll be off in you like a monster

I don't have too much to say

This time I'm guaranteed not to lose

Love sometimes can have you looking like a fool

Due to I worship the rain that falls on the grass that you walk on

You gotta a hold to my soul

So no matter what you're going through I always love you and that's just something that I want you to know

I love you so much

Wondering if you hear me when I pray for you

Things I remember through the pictures

I captured

You can blame me for whatever it is that caused you to fall through my fingers

But if I got you in my arms again

You'll be something I'd treasure

Memories is what keeps me holding on to you

I Sit Alone Sometimes

I sit alone sometimes and I think about you and
about all the fun we had and the things we used
to do
You never really gave us a chance to dance due to
the very second you got frustrated you planned
in advance
Your kisses I miss
Your touch I so wish
Wish that you would just touch me one last time
but the next time do it with a twist
If I could only go back
I'd grind you slower
And kiss your back at the same time
While caressing mind blind
I did everything right
But you wasn't used to that type of love right?
You'd rather me call you hoes and chase me while
I'm chasing those
That had nothing on you
Leave you in tears and broken
Is what you was used to
But I left you with a story you could tell
Like girrrrl

I can remember the way he used to touch me
Smile at me and tell me how much he used to
love me
I was that love who would open up car doors kiss
you in your sleep wake you up in the midnight
hour with my face in you, tasting you so sweet
Who is like me?
Name one person that can separate the lover from
the freak
That a pull your hair grip your throat
And in the next round I'm Denzel
Romancing so sweet
Who like me ?
Nobody
I bet you
You see my face whenever you're with him
When you see me on the outside
my presence shakes your soul
And curls your toes
I think about you from time to time
And can so admit
At times I can't get you off my mind
Loving the way you pillow bite
And we pillow fight
You are something I can't forget

I Wish We Could Be Alone

I wish we could be alone for a second

All I want is your conversation

Slow down for moment

I know you have a man

But he ain't got to know

He ain't on what I'm on

Yes he gots some nerve

Can I give you what you deserve?

Let's stop playing these games

Yes I can be a jokester

But you like that

Yes I can make your body shiver so bite down
right there and don't fight back

Can I play with your thoughts?

Due to in the mind

We can already have had one another

Just sitting here

Trust me pictures in the mind don't just fade away

Because once I'm in there

I'm not leaving til the next day

I want to work your body inside out

You know what I want and know what I need
There's so many things I want to do to you

Just open up and let me inside tonight

Ill knock three times

Before I enter

Just say the word

It a get better

I've been yearning to give my love

All this is natural

Can't nobody love you like I can

Leave

Excuse me Miss, I see you looking

Can I step up to you and try to paint this picture? Do you got a man because I won't carry on, I just thought I'd take the chance to ask before I took off home

See it's a good thing, but I didn't catch your name

see now I'm feeling your smile see I'm so glad you came

I see the floors like we're in the spot

Your body's hot

like fire, I had my eye on you as soon as I stepped through that door My eyes drop

Now I'm closer to you than before

Goose bumps all over my body just by imagining things I'd do to you

If you could read my mind, please don't ask

Due to I move a little fast, is this new to you?

You a sexy hotty

that can possibly have anybody

but your rocking with me

Let's have a private party

Yes I'm old school let's head to my place

you can hop inside your whip and follow me to
my upper floor where there's plenty of space

Baby let's taste every fruit that you can imagine

just say the word and I'll perform magic right in
your face

Let's go deep sea diving, rock climbing it's

One eighty-five on the dash

There's no need for seat belts because this ride is
going run safe and if we crash

We'll be on the floor off the dash

Finger sucking, toes curling, throat clutching

Deep loving

There's no need to close the door

we got all night alone until we're both sore.

I want you more even though I got you right here
with me right now

I want you even more when I wake up in you
high when the lights out

Do you like all the things that I'm whispering in
your ear?

Do my words touch your body, I want to feel you
here

Move in a little closer before the song goes off

Due to I want to take you there

Let's not care what others think, let them watch
while our imagination drink

Drink one another's wine

You can just say the word and we can ride

And I'll pop that secret lock to your door

And have you dreaming for more....

Do you want to leave...?

Pick Up The Pieces

I can tell you have a lot on your mind

Wishing you would just sit back and rewind

And let me in

I can make you forget all about him if only you let me pick up the pieces

I know just what you're missing

If you just pay attention and listen

I can be all the reasons that you smile

I don't want to be part of the problem

I'll never cheat or make you cry

Give you any reasons to why

He never knew what he had

But if you let me show you

I'll make you forget all about him

And the things he did

I need you to follow me

I want you...

Think about all the things that he did

And all the things he won't do

You make me move

You make me want to show you new

I can be all the things your heart dreamed to explore

And replace your past

Baby I'm about to lose it

I'm craving the way you used to move it

Move it in slow mo...

You'll never be sad

I'll replace the best you had

These are not only words

Close your eyes now feel me move

My aggressive is impassive

I want to make loving you more like a habit

I want you craving me like an addict

All the love from my past

I can admit

I possibly got enough practice

Now I think it's time

I'd let you have all this

Cause I'm not your average

She might tell you things about her experience with me

But you're not her and she's not you, and she refused to grow on my level but stuck on that savage

Trust me you know as well as I know

That I'm something in you that's missing

I want your mind

So can we switch positions?

And watch how easy this be you

Handing it to me and more

Pick your head up

Pick your head up love he wasn't worth it, she wasn't worth it, whatever. Let's cry together and heal one another we got this I can make you feel better. Let me love you mentally

Stand next to me

feel the intensity this could be

meant to me

Feel my whole energy taste this whole part of me...let's exchange juices

Mentally you are the epitome

I need

So don't feel you're worthless he never knew what he had just don't be that fool to turn

And look back

Let me be the reason

Your heart changes

Let me be the reason your heart sang

Ricky Boone

I want to be the one you smile in your sleep
thinking about when your eyes close

I want to be the reason your clothes fall off and
love exposes itself

So baby pick your head up

You're a queen

You're the scene of all majesty

Your apart of me

The heart of me I can't breathe, I can't see

I can't eat, so don't starve me Baby

Let us love

Let me into your mind don't look behind

Don't fall back

Look at life this is me

I'll sleep in you to finesse your peace

Take my soul inhale me dry

Look into my eyes be my high

Let us die in one another's arms

But with your teeth gripping locked to the sheets

And my head off into the fan blowing off the
sweat that drips gracefully off of me

Pick your head up and tell me don't you feel me,
I haven't even touched you yet

And I can feel you killing me

He ain't me and she isn't you

I'm a last of a dying breed

That's trying to grasp a hold to your burning
need

I want your heart, but give me your mind first

We'll never part because this love is real

And I'm forever dying of thirst

Don't be her... cause I damn sure ain't him

Pick your head up

Playing

Don't play like you don't see me looking ...due to the very second, we met, you had all my attention.

And out of all the women that was in the atmosphere,

It was just something about you that drew me near

Kind of bugged out

Trust me, this isn't like me, to be feeling this way

So I bet you think this is me just running some type of game,

To make you feel good like most niggaz but I'm in a different type of lane

I'm not going to play with you

I'm a give you me

Deadly word play, though but not today,

I got to give you the real me

Pillow Talk

No illusions no fantasies,

But me, is what I was thinking

Laughing to myself

Thinking on how much my appetite

Has changed towards women

I used to be in love with just booty and pretty
faces

That flooded my imagination, gave me the
greatest fetish to taste it

But now I yearn for nothing but a woman with a
conversation

I like that.

You don't have to do too much to impress me,

I'm digging your sexy

And the way your eyes undress me

I thank God for someone like you, he has really
blessed me.

It's really strange, that you desire to change, but
I don't complain

I love it just the same

A big girl, with a wig, or all natural

She's not only body

But got a brain, that could swallow knowledge

Will spit that wisdom off the deep end, if she has to, She doesn't care what people say about her size

As long as her man is satisfied

Isn't that right? All eyes on you and I know you feel them looking

But my eyes be the biggest, staring at all that Cushion

Blushing, rushing to get home just to get at you

Get in close the door I got everything you need,

There's no stopping, we on our way home,

I need all of you

Stop caring and thinking about what people say,

Your legs and thighs aren't too big, I'm the one loving you down this day

Let's go luv, the day is only beautiful because you're still in it

Why you running?

If I could only get you alone just to tell you how I really feel

maybe that a change something and cause your mindset to stand still

Wow baby, I think the last time we spoke you thought I was on some mess

And when I calmed you down, I figure you see I have more respect

You all quiet on the phone, me expressing my feelings saying baby I can't get you out my mind, I can't even play certain songs without wanting to tear up and cry

Wishing all your focus was really on me

Baby I never wanted you to give up

All I wanted you to do was to fill up on me

Pour a little bit more of me off into you

Waking up to you made me feel so brand new

missing you is something

I'm going through

And I bet you never had a love like this

And it's okay if you're afraid of this real spit

Wherever you're at is where I want to be

I don't want to miss no more of you

You is where I want to be

And loving you is no lie

But baby you're the only one that makes me feel like I can fly

The day that you parted from me, all I wanted to do was ball up and die

But you came back complicated

Drunk faded

And that's when I knew I should of pulled back because love doesn't confuse

So that's why I didn't trip

I shouldn't of given you all of that good

But just given you the very tip of wood

I didn't want to look like a chaser or slouch

But I still have memories

Of you crossed up like a pretzel on the couch

Baby my thoughts play like a movie

I stay on play, it moves me

Soothes me, grooves me.

Ooooweee

I know you haven't had a love like me before

Even though I wanted to run back and catch
your tears the very second I slammed the car door

Can I pour a little bit of me back off into you?

I know you miss it

Lady can we start over like new?

Why you running....

About The Author

Born in Saginaw Michigan but raised in Grand Rapids Michigan, Ricky Boone discovered his passion for writing when he was 14 years old. He attempted to write his first book based on his love for movies.

"I've always seen part two and three even before they were created. However, I watched a movie called 'Under the Cherry Moon' by Prince, and the poetry he wrote in the movie inspired me, and I've been hooked ever since."

Author Ricky Boone links into many poets such as Desiree Renea, a poet that was dedicated into ministry in the church. She introduced him, and he stood up in front of the congregation. Later on, he started following Black Ice, which was another poet as well that gave Ricky Boone the push he needed.

Afterwards he joined a group on Facebook called The Inner Circle, which was ran by Kesha Murphy and king Judah. Both were erotic and love poets who asked Ricky to collaborate with them, which sparked a flame that drew him into a totally new audience.

This eventually caused Ricky Boone to start writing out his emotions and experiences. "Through my marriages, whether it was on a positive or negative level, I figured why give up on love; because it hasn't given up on me. I started to desire certain things, wanting to share with that special person, and thought well...I know I can't be the only one who desires these things. By the end of my divorce in 2017, which I thought would have broken me, I learned to channel that pain into what I wanted in a woman, and how I wanted her to treat me. And that was the birth of pillow talk."

To learn more about Author Ricky Boone and his upcoming works and poetic expressions, visit the publishing website.

www.AJBPublishing.com

www.ingramcontent.com/pod-product-compliance
Lightning Source LLC
Chambersburg PA
CBHW021223090426
42740CB00006B/345